PERLAS NIN SIRANGAN

Narratives of Bicolano Learners on Patriotism

by

Jerilyn M. Torio, Ed. D

COPYRIGHT © 2021 PERLAS NIN SIRANGAN:
Narratives of Bicolano Learners on Patriotism
By Jerilyn M. Torio, Ed. D

Edited by Marie Ezekiel
Designed by Tess Ritumalta

ISBN:
Hardbound-978-621-470-118-6
Mobile/Kindle-978-621-470-119-3
Softbound/Paperback-978-621-470-120-9

Published by:
Poetry Planet Book Publishing House
Rosario, Pozorrubio, Pangasinan, Philippines
Contact No.: 09554960044
Email: maritesritumalta@gmail.com

PREFACE

For more than a decade now, I worked as a teacher, and during the first day of my meeting with my class, I always request my students to write the lyrics of the Philippine National Anthem with a time frame of seven (7) minutes. It is truly an alarming situation for me as a music teacher that as years passed by, students' patriotism is diminishing.

There are a lot of issues regarding the singing of the Philippine National Anthem even in international events. Singers and performers seldom make a mistake by changing the lyrics and rendition of the song. Filipinos should recover and revitalize the lost and faded values of "love for the country". It is the responsibility of every Filipino citizen to cultivate and continuously reinforce a strong sense of citizenship and nationhood by appreciating and understanding our national symbols.

The purpose of this book is to strengthen the patriotism of the students and assist the MAPEH (Music, Art, Physical Education, and Health) and AP (Araling Panlipunan) in teaching the students in writing, singing, and deepening their understanding of the Philippine National Anthem.

"Lupang Hinirang" is our height of honor and every Filipino must be proud of.

INTRODUCTION

Patriotism is a devotion to one's country for no other reason than being a citizen of that country. It is a common virtue that pertains to the love for a nation, with more emphasis on values and beliefs.

Knowing the national anthem and showing how it is properly sung is one way of displaying respect and love for the country. However, in research conducted, it was found out that students' patriotism is diminishing while assessing their writing, singing, and understanding of the Philippine national anthem.

As a preventive measure and remedy of producing an ignorant Filipino citizen in the future, teachers, as well as the parents, should go hand in hand in patiently teaching the love for the country to their kids. In addition to this, teachers from pre-elementary to high school or even colleges and universities should spend ample time not only in teaching the Lupang Hinirang but oblige every student to memorize the lyrics of the song by stressing out the correct title and rendition of the national anthem during their Araling Panlipunan, MAPEH, or Music subjects. Thus, making every Filipino citizen realize that memorizing the National Anthem is a duty and responsibility to our country.

TABLE OF CONTENTS

CHAPTER I

INTRODUCTION

Patriotism is a devotion to one's country for no other reason than being a citizen of that country. It is a common virtue that pertains to the love for a nation, with more emphasis on values and beliefs. One who is patriotic will be ready to make any sacrifice for his country. He will never live selfishly for himself alone. A soldier for instance makes that supreme sacrifice of his life for the sake of his country. The famous poet Rabindranath Tagore, (Dapula, 2015) himself a great patriot, said that a patriot loves his own country, but he does not hate the people of other countries. You may call yourself a patriot if you consider to respect the flag, value Filipino identity, know your nation's history, and be able to share it with others.

In the Philippines, today, we are lacking in patriots largely due to the diffusion of Filipino values, culture, influence, and the confluence of historical bad governance. Schools must have the best platform for instilling such values to the students; teachers must impart the gospel of patriotism to remind this day's generation that the fight for freedom of the Katipuneros is a continuing struggle that we are still fighting for. Modern heroes – teachers, uniformed men, public servants must be encouraged to rekindle the spirit of patriotism that lived in our heroes 120 years ago. Department of Education should give also importance on how nationalism be engraved to Filipino youth. According to Malipot (2018), the Department of Education will continue its campaign for greater awareness on patriotism and valor among learners and its own personnel through various activities. The department has activities and celebrations aimed to instill in the minds and hearts of the Filipino people, that the freedom the Filipinos enjoy today was nourished by the blood and sacrifices of the veteran forefathers. Filipinos are among the most patriotic people in the world. Pledge to the flag and singing of the national anthem is a simple gesture and manifestation of every Filipino's love of country.

In her article, Carag (2018) stated that Manny Pacquiao, World Boxing Champion, said that there are some Filipinos betraying the country and disrespecting the Philippine National Anthem. According to Isip (2015), Filipinos in majority don't even remember the lyrics of the song. The truth is, they know how to sing it but frequently use other terms because they were not passionately taught and supervised during their formal years of schooling. In a television show, a person once asked by this question: "Ano ang Awit ng Pilipinas?" Then he answered, "Bayang Magiliw"! Unbelievable but true. Even in school setting, this kind of circumstances is really happening wherein most pupils frequently commit errors in identifying the title of our National Anthem.

According to Basas (Carag, 2018), it is not fair to put the blame solely on the teachers and the educational system. The Teachers Dignity Coalition official explained that the development of a child is affected by other factors, including family, community, and religion. He further insisted that public schools are already teaching their students to respect the national anthem, other national symbols, and the Filipino

language as manifestations of patriotism. Meanwhile, the TDC head said that they support the proposal of Pacquiao to enhance the teaching of patriotism in public schools, but believes that the creation of a separate subject is not needed, and it could be integrated into other subjects.

As a preventive measure and remedy of producing ignorant Filipino citizens in the future, teachers, as well as the parents, should go hand and hand in patiently teaching the correct lyrics and rendition of the song. In addition to this, the song should be taught as early as the formative schooling years of the child. Teachers from the pre-elementary to high school or even state colleges should spend ample time not only in teaching the song but also to oblige every pupil to memorize the lyrics of "Lupang Hinirang" by stressing out the correct title and rendition of the song during their MAPEH, or music subjects. Thus, making every Filipino citizen realize that memorizing the National Anthem is a duty and responsibility to our country.

RESEARCH OBJECTIVES

This study narrated the personal experiences of the Bicolano junior high school learners and teachers in singing, writing, and understanding the Philippine National Anthem using the Narrative Inquiry and Phenomenological Analysis C/Y 2019-2020.

Specifically, this study aimed to achieve the following objectives:

1. Narrate the personal experiences of Bicolano learners and teachers in singing, writing, and understanding the National Anthem using the Narrative Inquiry and Phenomenological Analysis.

2. Develop a module promoting national pride.

SCOPE AND DELIMITATION

This study used the narrative inquiry and phenomenological approach which looked into the personal experiences of Bicolano learners and teachers in writing, singing, and understanding the Philippine national anthem.

Respondents were students and teachers from the selected secondary schools of Naga City Division and Division of Camarines Sur namely: Camarines Sur National High School, Sipocot National High School, Sta. Lutgarda National High School, Milaor National High School, and Calabanga National High School during the SY 2019-2020.

Observation instruments were used to evaluate the students' performance in singing the Lupang Hinirang during flag ceremonies. Students were also requested to write the Lupang Hinirang with a given time frame of five (5) to seven (7) minutes. Solo singing was also done by selected students from the five schools. Focused group discussion was also observed in the study.

THEORETICAL FRAMEWORK

The Patriotism Theory served as the main theory that provided direction in this study, supported by Gellner's Theory of Nationalism, Lustig's Cultural Identity Theory, Republic Act No. 8491, and DepEd Order #50, s. 2015.

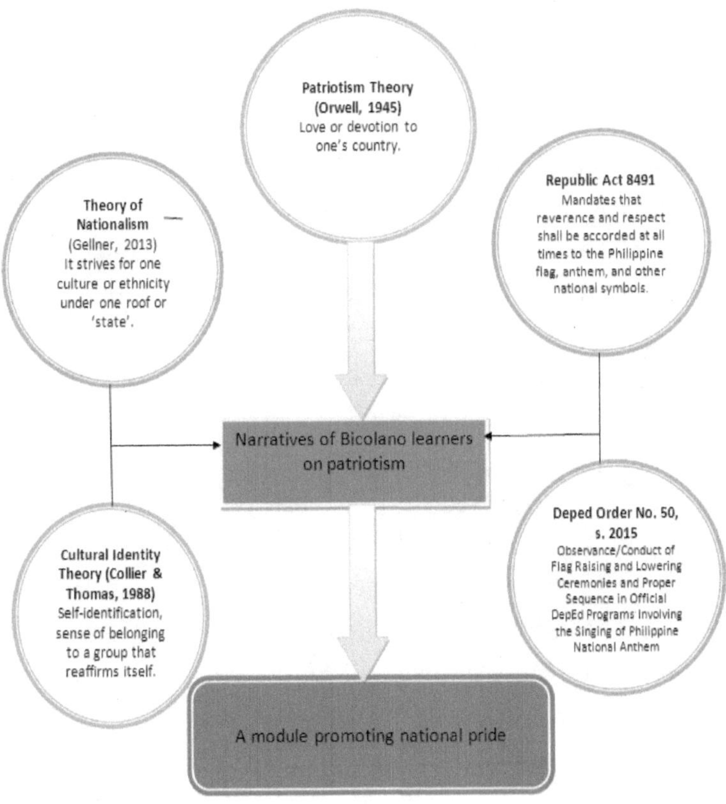

Figure 1.1 Theoretical Model of the Study

Patriotism defines as the "love of one's country". This captures the core meaning of the term in ordinary use, but it might well be thought too thin and in need of fleshing out. Stephen Nathanson (1993, 34-35) defines patriotism as involving: (1) special affection for one's own country; (2) a sense of personal identification with the country; (3) special concern for the well-being of the country; and (4) willingness to sacrifice to promote the country's good.

Gellner's Theory of Nationalism was developed by Ernest Gellner over a number of publications from around the early 1960s to his 1995 death. Gellner discussed nationalism in several works and he most notably developed it in Nations and Nationalism in 1983. He defined nationalism as "primarily a political principle which holds that the political and the national unit should be congruent and as the general imposition of a high culture on society, where previously low cultures had taken up the lives of the majority and in some cases the totality, of the population. It means the general diffusion of a school-mediated, academy-supervised idiom, codified for the requirements of reasonably precise bureaucratic and technological communication. It is the establishment of an anonymous impersonal society, with mutually sustainable atomized individuals, held together above all by a shared culture of this kind, in place of the previous complex structure of local groups, sustained by folk cultures reproduced locally and idiosyncratically by the micro-groups themselves.

Nationalism is a political, social, and economic ideology and movement characterized by the promotion of the interests of a particular nation, especially with the aim of gaining and

maintaining the nation's sovereignty over its homeland. Nationalism holds that each nation should govern itself, free from outside interference, that a nation is the only rightful source of political power. It further aims to build and maintain a single national identity – based on shared social characteristics such as culture, language, religion, politics, and belief in a shared singular history – and to promote national unity or solidarity. Nationalism, therefore, seeks to preserve and foster a nation's traditional culture, and cultural revivals have been associated with nationalist movements. It also encourages pride in national achievements and is closely linked to patriotism.

According to Lustig (2013), cultural identity refers to a person's sense of belonging to a particular culture or group. This process involves learning about and accepting traditions, heritage, language, religion, ancestry, aesthetics, thinking patterns, and social structures of culture. Normally, people internalize the beliefs, values, norms, and social practices of their culture and identify themselves with that culture. The culture becomes part of their self-concept. However, some studies have noted that existing cultural identity theory may not account for the fact that different individuals and groups may not react to or interpret events, happenings, attitudes, etc. in the same ways as other individuals or groups.

Myron Lustig notes that cultural identities are central to a person's sense of self. That is because cultural identities are central, dynamic, and multifaceted components of one's self-concept. He also points out that cultural identities are dynamic, and they exist within a changing social context. As a result, a person's identity changes as do one's ongoing experiences in life. Other researchers describe cultural identity as referring to the content of values as guiding principles, to meaningful symbols, and to lifestyles that individuals share with others though not necessarily within recognizable groups. Cultural identity is defined as the identity of a group or culture or of an individual as far as one is influenced by one's belonging to a group or culture.

Cultural identity is self-identification, a sense of belonging to a group that reaffirms itself. It is the extent to which one is representative of a given culture behaviorally, communicatively, psychologically, and sociologically. It consists of values, meanings, customs, and beliefs used to relate to the world. It reflects the common historical experiences and shared cultural codes which give us as one entity a stable, unchanging, continuing frame of reference and meaning. People's judgments about whether they or others belong to a cultural group can be influenced by physical appearance, ancestral origin, or personal behavior. A historical event, political conditions, who is present, situation of interaction, and public discourse, also affect cultural identity. Cultural identity is dynamic and constantly evolving. It covers the entire life span of a human being and changes every moment based on social context. Cultural identity is the constantly shifting understanding of one's identity in relation to others.

Republic Act No. 8491, also known as "The Flag and Heraldic Code of the Philippines", is amended to highlight the importance of complying, abiding, and conforming to the standard expression as prescribed by law. Every citizen of a country has the moral obligation to love its motherland. Our 1987 Constitution mandates this obligation. In our country, such national symbols like the national flag, anthem, motto, coat-of-arms, and other heraldic items and devices are the representation of the Philippines. Thus, it is innate to every Filipino to respect, learn it and live by it.

Pursuant to Section 18 of Republic Act (RA) No. 8491, otherwise known as the "Flag and Heraldic Code of the Philippines", all government offices and educational institutions are required to participate in the Observance/Conduct of Flag Raising Ceremonies every Monday morning and Flag Lowering Ceremonies every Friday afternoon. This is one of the highlights in the DepEd Order No. 50, s. 2015 entitled "Observance/Conduct of Flag Raising and Lowering Ceremonies and Proper Sequence in Official DepEd Programs Involving the Singing of the Philippine National Anthem dated October 29, 2015.

CONCEPTUAL FRAMEWORK

The conceptual framework that guided this study is depicted in a paradigm shown in Figure 2.

Philippine National Anthem is sung as early as the pupils enroll in their nursery level; sometimes earlier than that, taught by parents, relatives, or teachers.

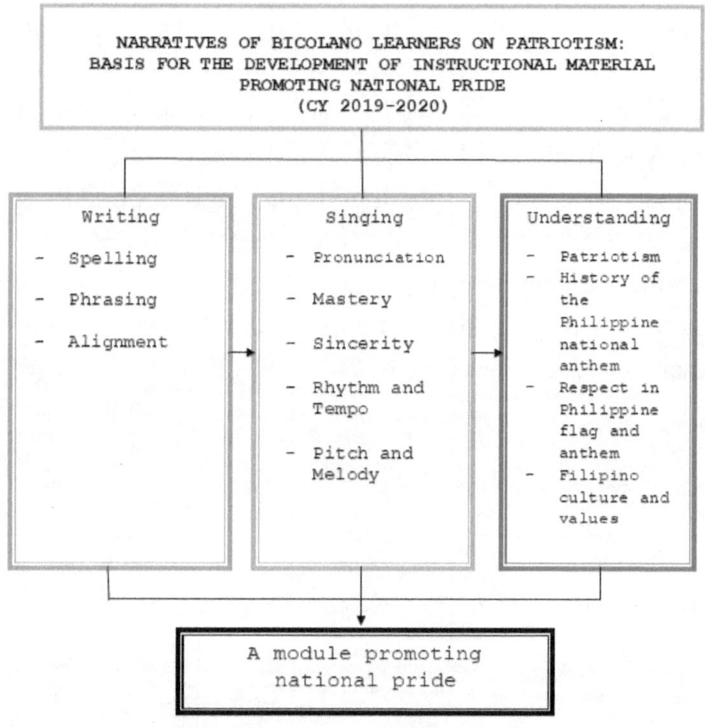

Figure 2. Conceptual Paradigm (Illustrating the Relationship Between Narratives of Bicolano Learners on

patriotism in the manner of writing, singing and understanding the Philippine National Anthem)

However, it is not taught word by word and Filipino terms are not explained to pupils about its meaning and how it is used in the song. Teachers sometimes post the lyrics of the song on the board, let the students read it, and let them listen to the song. Frequently, teachers rely on the singing of Lupang Hinirang during flag ceremonies and let the students listen to it while there is a song leader or music. Well, in fact, there are so many students who do not know how to write, sing and don't even understand the meaning of the song and how it should be sung.

Factors in writing, singing, and understanding the Philippine national anthem will be discussed following the themes collected in the study.

<u>ASSUMPTIONS</u>

Students are singing the National Anthem everyday with pride and dignity as a Filipino since it is taught in schools during the first year of each division level.

DEFINITION OF TERMS

This section presents the terms defined conceptually and operationally for a better understanding of how these terms will be used.

ALIGNMENT. This refers to how the students write the lyrics of the Philippine National Anthem in proper alignment and stanza according to the features and characteristics of a poem. It refers to the arrangement in a straight line, correct or appropriate positions of words in writing the lyrics of the Lupang Hinirang.

BICOLANO LEARNERS. This refers to the junior high school students of the five secondary schools of the Division of Camarines Sur where the research and observations were conducted. Additionally, it refers to the students who attended the Focused Group Discussion and express their experiences in writing, singing, and understanding of Lupang Hinirang.

LUPANG HINIRANG. This refers to the title of the Philippine National Anthem composed by Julian Felipe in 1898, and the lyrics were adapted from the Spanish poem Filipinas, written by Jose Palma in 1899. The Spanish lyrics were translated into Tagalog beginning in the 1940s, with the current Filipino version from 1956 undergoing a slight version in the 1960s.

MASTERY. This refers to memorization of the Philippine National Anthem from its pitch, rhythmic pattern, tempo, and other elements in music to the mastery of all the terms present in the lyrics of the Lupang Hinirang.

<u>NARRATIVE.</u> This refers to presenting or understanding a situation while students and teachers tell their experiences during the conduct of Flag Ceremonies. It was accurately done during the Focused Group Discussion where students and teachers gathered together to describe their practices and understanding of Lupang Hinirang.

<u>NATIONAL PRIDE</u>. This comprises the national symbols of the Philippines including the Philippine flag, national anthem, and other national symbols. This study refers to the Philippine National Anthem where Filipinos should give respect and reverence while singing and listening.

<u>PATRIOTIC SONG.</u> This refers to a song with patriotic content; it can be the national anthem of a country, nationalistic songs with the theme of love for the country. It evokes feelings of national fervor and pride of what the people are and what they represent, as a great nation.

<u>PATRIOTISM.</u> This refers to the quality of being patriotic; love and devotion to and vigorous support for one's country. It is also called national pride which refers to the feeling of love, devotion, and sense of attachment which can be a combination of different feelings relating to one's homeland, including ethnic, cultural, political, or historical aspects.

<u>PITCH AND MELODY</u>. This refers to proper tune while singing the Lupang Hinirang. It is also important to listen to the pitch given by the conductor so that singing of the Philippine National Anthem is sung in monophonic texture or has only the same pitch even though composed of many singers or people.

<u>PHRASING.</u> A substantial musical thought which can emphasize a concept in the music or message in the lyrics.

Similar to a phrase in grammar, it defines a group of words that express a complete musical concept which refers to the act or method of resulting the grouped notes into musical phrases.

PRONUNCIATION. This refers to how students articulate each lyric of the Philippine National Anthem depending on how they know and memorize the terms. Most of the students only murmur during the singing of the Lupang Hinirang.

SINCERITY. This refers to giving respect, reverence, and importance to national pride and other national symbols; giving the highest esteem to the national flag and anthem during the conduct of Flag Ceremonies.

RHYTHM AND TEMPO. This refers to the rendition of the national anthem in accordance with the original composition and arrangement of Julian Felipe which is in march tempo, in 2-4 time signature having a range of 100-120 metronome.

SINGING. This refers to the Philippine National Anthem while singing with the right palm is placed over the left chest. Uniformed personnel, meanwhile, are to sauté the flag as prescribed by their respective regulations. House Bill 5224 specifies the proper rendition of "Lupang Hinirang" in accordance with the musical arrangement and composition of Julian Felipe: 2/4 beat when played, within the range of 100 to 120 metronome, in 4/4 beat when sang.

SPELLING. It defines as the process or activity of writing each lyric or Filipino word present in the Philippine national anthem. Since the Philippine national anthem is now translated into Filipino, it is expected that students can write and understand each term in the lyrics in the correct spelling.

WRITING. This refers to a process or a medium of human communication that is used to recognize the students' level of awareness of the correct spelling, phrasing, and alignment of the Philippine national anthem. Writing is one of the activities conducted to evaluate the students' writing aspect of the Lupang Hinirang.

UNDERSTANDING. It refers to the appreciation and knowledge of the Philippine national anthem; its background and how Filipinos should behave during the conduct of Flag Ceremonies showing patriotism and love for the country. It may refer to a fact, information, and skills acquired by a Filipino citizen through practical understanding and awareness of the Philippine national anthem.

NOTES

Jose Paulo Dapula. (2015)."Patriotism and Nationalism." Retrieved from https://www.slideshare.net/100000861051472/patriotism-and-nationalism#:~:text=Nationalism%20The%20famous%20poet%20Rabindranath,the%20people%20of%20other%20nations.

Merlina Hernando-Malipot (2018). "DepEd to continue campaign for greater awareness on patriotism, valor among learners, personnel." Retrieved from https://mb.com.ph/2018/04/30/deped-to-continue-campaign-for-greater-awareness-on-patriotism-valor-among-learners-personnel/

Kristan Carag (2018). "Teachers' group deflects blame for 'lack of patriotism in society." Retrieved from https://dzrhnews.com.ph/teachers-group-deflects-blame-lack-patriotism-society/

Froilan G. Isip (2015). "Philippine National Anthem: Bayang Magiliw?" Retrieved from https://www.pressreader.com/philippines/sunstar-pampanga/20150325/281625303796790

Wang & Jia. (2015). "The Contemporary Value of Patriotism." Retrieved from https://file.scirp.org/pdf/AASoci_2015051414401558.pdf

Daniel Druckman. (2010). "Nationalism, Patriotism, and Group Loyalty: A Psychological Perspective." Retrieved from http://bev.berkeley.edu/Ethnic%20Religious%20Conflict/Ethnic%20and%20Religious%20Conflict/2%20National%20Identity/Druckman%20nationalism.pdf

Margaret Louise Costelo. (2009). "The Filipino Ringside Community: National Identity and the Heroic Myth of Manny Pacquiao." Retrieved from https://repository.library.georgetown.edu/bitstream/handle/10822/552909/costelloMargaret.pdf?seq

Haidee C. Pineda. "The Arts and Philippine Studies." *UPDate Magazine. 4 (1);18.* University of the Philippines Publication, Diliman, Quezon City.

Neal D. Mathene. (2014). "Naming the Artist, Composing the Philippines: Listening for the Nation in the National Artist Award." Retrieved from https://escholarship.org/content/qt5bc31081/qt5bc31081.pdf

Yea-Wen Chen and Hengjun Lin. "Cultural Identities." Retrieved from https://oxfordre.com/communication/view/10.1093/acrefore/9780190228613.001.0001/acrefore-9780190228613-e-20?print=pd

Republic Act No. 8491

DepEd Order No. 50, s. 2015

CHAPTER II

REVIEW OF LITERATURE AND STUDIES

This chapter presents the related readings which start with literature on patriotism and the second section centers on previously conducted studies on patriotism, nationalism, and national anthems. The last part synthesizes the review.

RELATED LITERATURE

Col. Noel Detoyato in the article of Nepomuceno (2019) reiterated that a mandatory Reserve Officers' Training Corps (ROTC) program will help instill the need and value of protecting the nation to the youth. He cleared out that the AFP believes it is time to bring back mandatory ROTC in schools to ensure that the youth are shaped with a deep sense of patriotism and love for the country. Since protecting the nation is a concern of every citizen, mandatory ROTC enrolment will instill this to the youth.

Department of Education (DepEd) Secretary Leonor Magtolis Briones (2019) underscored the importance of strengthening global citizenship in achieving the education targets set by various international organizations including the United Nations, the United Nations Educational, Scientific, and Cultural Organization (UNESCO), the Asia-Pacific Economic Cooperation (APEC), and the Southeast Asian Ministers of

Education Organization (SEAMEO), among others. Briones further enjoined the participants to love their own communities and countries, while keeping in mind that they are part of a broader community, region, and of the planet Earth.

Rocamora (2018) believed that ordinary Filipinos whom President Duterte described as "everyday heroes" are regarded as the country's "modern-day heroes" for the sacrifice they give to provide for their families and also to keep the economy afloat. Whether one helps directly or indirectly or saves a thousand or a single person, anyone who helps promote the welfare of another is a hero – someone deserving of respect and gratitude. They are everywhere but you may not just recognize or acknowledge them. They are silent and the humble who finish their jobs without much exaltation; they are all in our midst.

Senator Loren Legarda (2018) has called on the youth to emulate Dr. Jose Rizal's patriotism, and unequivocal dedication to fight for the protection and preservation of the Filipino heritage, as the nation commemorates the national hero's 157th birth anniversary on June 19, 2018. She said that the values and principles of Jose Rizal as the country's national hero have been instilled in all Filipinos. She encouraged the youth to emulate Rizal's indisputable loyalty and love for the country and for people's heritage as the fate and future of the Philippines. She added that the progress and freedom that Rizal's fought for the Filipinos are still the very same challenges the Filipinos are facing. Moreover, Legarda renewed her call for the Filipino youth to respect and preserve the nation's heritage, stressing that Rizal himself had expressed the need to embrace one's roots.

Singson, as indicated in the article of De Leon (2018), urged the Overseas Filipino Workers (OFWs) often referred to as the country's Modern Day heroes to follow the steps of Jose Rizal, the Philippine national hero who fought and died for the country's freedom for colonialism. He also told the OFWs to be a model residents and represent the Philippines well to the host country where they are working.

Patriotism, love of country, love for country, sense of pride of place, whatever we may want to call, it is not responsibility of the school or community alone, and as with charity, also should begin at home. It was stressed out by Pangilinan (2018) that, one of the best ways to cultivate patriotism in young children is through songs and folkslore. Parents must not wait until a child goes to school to learn our folksongs or legends, but introduce them in our daily life. She added that we can raise kids who are not only globally competitive but are good Filipinos too.

Katipunan (2017) stated that the House of Representatives approved on third and final reading by a unanimous vote of 212-0 House Bill 5224, which updates, among others, the rules on the rendition of the National Anthem, expressly repealing Republic Act 8491 on the Flag and Heraldic Code of the Philippines. She explained that HB 5224 ostensibly has the laudable objective to inculcate in the minds and hearts of people. She was also surprised to learn that the Philippines has a national motto – "Maka-Diyos, Maka-Tao, Makakalikasan at Makabansa", which was also found in the Old Flag Law, Republic Act 8491, Section 40. Furthermore, HB 5224 specifically provides for the correct rendition and manner of singing of the Philippine National Anthem. She also discussed that the wrong rendition and manner of singing of "Lupang Hinirang" is not only a ground for the administrative discipline of all government officials and employees, but any person can go to jail for up to one year and/or pay a fine of not less than P50,000 nor more than P100,000 if convicted (Section 49, HB 5224).

In his inaugural speech, President Duterte (cited by Hernandez, 2016) called on everyone to recover and revitalize the lost and faded values of "love of country, subordination of personal interests to the common good, concern and care for the helpless and the impoverished." Whether Mr. Duterte realizes it or not, the task of cultivating and continuously reinforcing a strong sense of citizenship and nationhood in generations of Filipinos rests on two places: our homes and our schools.

To repeal RA 8491, otherwise known as the "Flag and Heraldic Code of the Philippines", in the light of contemporary changes in attitudes and idioms, and to instill love of country and underscore the importance of complying with standard expressions of respect for our national symbols, Rep. Rodriguez (2017) introduced the Revised Flag and Heraldic Code otherwise known as House Bill 5224. It has nineteen (19) key provisions and was approved by the Committee Affairs Department of House of Representatives on January 31, 2017.

Patriotism is a ten-letter word that is so vague but has a deeper feeling of pride to people who clearly understand what

it really signifies. Modern generation nowadays, especially the 21st-century learners, don't have any idea how significant the word patriotism is and how important it is to introduce it to the learners. According to Paras (2016), patriotism is showing love for one's country, being proud of your nationality or where one came from, and standing still even if the world is against you. She posed a question on how can the teacher help in inculcating patriotism to learners? According to her, there are four ways in how educators can instill patriotism in learners. First, teaching children patriotic songs. Children love songs and rhymes. These songs and rhymes can be embedded in their tender hearts. Second, ceremonial use of patriotic words and songs in the school programs, scouting ceremonies, and community sports openings and closings, and other social activities can inspire children to grow patriotic. Third, arrange patriotic programs that educators, in particular, can get many opportunities to fuel patriotism through school programs. Lastly, having a discussion during school debates can provide children the opportunity to hear issues, and to participate in the discussions about important concerns.

RELATED STUDIES

Bernardo (2017) conducted to study political values of Filipinos. An etic approach was adopted using as a starting point the theory of core political values to explore the political values of a sample of 699 Filipinos who participated in an online survey. The results of explanatory and confirmatory factor analytic procedures suggest three core political values –

conservation, globalism, equal rights – that have distinct motivational directions.

Sardoc (2017) explained that both historically and conceptually, patriotism has been one of the foundational characteristics that define the very essence of one's attachment, identification, and loyalty to a political community that is a basic virtue associated with citizenship as a political conception of the person. His study examined some of the foundational elements associated with the discussion of patriotism.

Nair and Sinasamy (2017) determined the relationship between patriotism and students' interests in learning history. Findings indicated that there was no significant difference in students' mean scores for patriotism according to gender and subject streams. In addition, the findings also showed that there was a significant correlation between the students' mean score for patriotism and their interest towards learning History. These findings have strong theoretical, pedagogical, and practical implications. In terms of theoretical implication, the findings support constitutional patriotism by Muller. In terms of practical implications, teachers should employ the right strategies and use effective teaching materials to enhance students' interest and understanding of History which will also help to enhance their level of patriotism. In terms of practical implications Ministry of Education, Teachers Training Division, and other stakeholders should find ways to unite the young generation by bridging their gap in patriotism.

According to Teehankee (2016), Filipino nationalism is constructed upon a history of opposition to a colonial and alien 'other". By reviving the anti-US nationalism of his youth, Duterte is repudiating the liberal reformist, albeit elitist, a narrative of the Aquino-to-Aquino regime. In his study, Sison said that he and President Duterte are both inspired by the principles and objectives of Kabataang Makabayan and driven by the patriotic desire to continue the unfinished revolution of Andres Bonifacio.

Ozturk, et. al (2016) defined patriotism using the concepts like love, loyalty, and responsibility. Teachers emphasized love for and loyalty to the country as the most significant indicator of patriotism. They explained this within the context of awareness of history, sharing a common culture, independence, and territorial integrity. It was also stressed out that today, students are not interested in patriotism, and students do not have the sense of patriotism as they used to have when they were students. Teachers think that students' sense of patriotism is not enough, which has different reasons. Participating teachers thought that individuals' values of patriotism and behaviors are nourished more by national and historical awareness.

Castillo, et. al (2016) investigated the socio-demographic characteristics of the Filipino youth in the National Capital Region and how it is related to the level of national pride in domain-specific aspects of the respondents among their socio-demographic characteristics. In their study, it was discovered that there is not one authentic Philippine date in history until 1521, the year when the Spaniards arrived in the Philippines, bringing Christianity. This showed how history co-existed with religion in the Philippines. As the friars taught the Filipinos

Christianity, they also embedded in us to save memorable dates and give value to history.

Ho (2016) compared interactions between social changes and the integration of nationalism and multiculturalism in the context of music education by focusing on the ways in which the governmental politics of mainland China and the United States have managed nationalism and diversity in school music education. His paper argued that music education, as seen in these two countries, can be continually reinvented through the interplay between nationalism and multiculturalism in response to changing needs and contexts.

According to Their (2016), global citizenship literature has been diffuse, featuring multiple definitions, at least 140 extant measures, and potential overlaps 11 other constructs. He combined findings from content analysis of qualitative data with results of exploratory and confirmatory factor analyses of survey data, reporting the extent to which students' and teachers' understanding of global citizenship confirms, complements, and contradicts the behavior of three measures that purport to tap global citizenship. Results provide evidence that work is needed, likely partnering researchers and educators before there is a high school-ready measure of global citizenship.

Wang and Jia (2015) concluded that patriotism is a kind of emotion that will be thought theory and behavior as a whole. The reaction of the complex relationship between individuals and country value system is formed in the process of social history, and it is developed and consolidated in the process of human society, it is a kind of thought and feeling of loyalty and loves their motherland. With the development of the era, patriotism has a deeper meaning. In the prevailing of peace and development today, every country competes with other countries hotly, so patriotism will have more contemporary values.

STATE-OF-THE-ART

The following are a summary of the related literature. Detoyato (2019) and Secretary Briones (2019) underscored the importance of instilling patriotism in the minds of the youth. It was also mentioned by Legarda (2018) to emulate Dr. Rizal's patriotism and love for the country. She pushed the Filipino youth to respect and preserve the nation's heritage, stressing that Rizal himself had expressed the need to embrace one's roots. Pangilinan (2018) also stressed the importance of cultivating patriotism in young children inside their homes. In addition to this, it is also taught in schools since it is also a part of the DepEd motto: Maka-Diyos, Maka-Tao, Makakalikasan at Makabansa. President Duterte (Hernandez, 2016) called on everyone to recover and revitalize the lost and faded values of "love of country". He also described every Filipino as "everyday hero", one who promotes the welfare of another. It was also mentioned (De Leon, 2018) that the country's modern-day heroes are the Overseas Filipino Workers though they are working abroad. They have a deeper feeling of pride and love for the country and serve as model residents and represent the Philippines well to the host country they are working.

Meanwhile, Sardo (2017) and Nair and Sinasamy (2017) concluded that patriotism has one of the foundational characteristics that define the importance of one's attachment to his or her country. History plays an important aspect in teaching patriotism to people. By reviving Filipino nationalism (Teehankee, 2016), the young people will be driven by a patriotic desire to continue the unfinished business of our heroes. It was also explained by Ozturk, et.al (2016) that within the context of awareness of history, love and loyalty to the country is the most significant indicator of patriotism. It was also concluded by Wang and Jia (2015) that patriotism is a kind of emotion that will think of theory and behavior as a whole.

The previous studies featured differently to the present study. The uniqueness of this study is a narration of Bicolano learners on patriotism as a basis for developing a module promoting national pride. It centers on the writing, singing, and understanding of the Philippine National Anthem of the secondary students and how the Lupang Hinirang should be taught and addressed in schools specifically in Araling Panlipunan and MAPEH subjects. Additionally, module was developed that provides activities that will engage the students and teachers on how the Philippine National Anthem can be taught in schools so that students will strengthen their patriotism and love for the country.

NOTES

Priam Nepomuceno. (2019). "Mandatory ROTC Necessary to Instill Patriotism Among Youth." Philippine News Agency. Retrieved from https://www.pna.gov.ph/articles/1061627.

DepEd. (2018). "Briones: Strengthening Global Citizenship Key to Achieving Education Goals 2030." Retrieved from https://pia.gov.ph/news/articles/1012912

Joyce Ann L. Rocamora. (2018). "OFWs: Modern-day Heroes Still." Philippine News Agency. https://www.pna.gov.ph/articles/1046084

"Legarda Encourages Filipino Youth to Emulate Rizal's Patriotism, Love for Culture and Environment." Retrieved from June 19, 2018. http://www.senate.gov.ph/press_release/2018/0619_legarda1.asp

Janice Ponce De Leon. (2018). "Filipinos Parade their Patriotism, Positive Spirit."Retrieved from https://gulfnews.com/going-out/society/filipinos-parade-their-patriotism-positive-spirit-1.2237250

Ching Pangilinan. (2018). "Cultivating Patriotism." Sun Star Pampanga.Retrieved from https://www.sunstar.com.ph/article/1747239

Atty. Lorna Patajo-Katipunan. (2017). "Criminalizing 'not singing with fervor'!." Retrieved from
https://businessmirror.com.ph/criminalizing-not-singing-with-fervor/

Butch Hernandez. (2016). "A Better, Safer and Kinder Nation. " Philippine Daily Inquirer Retrieved from https://opinion.inquirer.net/95678/a-better-safer-and-kinder-nation

"HB 5224." (January 31, 2017.) Retrieved from http://www.congress.gov.ph/legisdocs/first_17/CR00163.pdf

Maria Jonelle T. Paras. (2016). "Inculcating Patriotism among Learners." Sun   Star Pampanga. Retrieved from   https://www.pressreader.com/

Allan B.I. Bernardo. (2017). "Exploring Political Values of Filipinos Using an Etic Approach." University of Macau. Taipa,   Macau.Retrieved   from https://www.pap.org.ph/sites/default/files/upload/pjp2017-50-2-pp7-38-bernardo-exploring_political_values_of_filipi   nos using_an_etic_approach.pdf

Mitja Sardoc. (2017). "The Anatomy of Patriotism." Retrieved   from https://www.researchgate.net/publication/317688502_The_anat omy_of_patriotism

Subadrah Madhawa Nair and Rajeswary P. Sinasamy. "Patriotism among Secondary School Students and Its Relationship with their Interests towards Learning History." Asian Journal of Education and Training. 3 (2); 110-117.

Julio C. Teehankee. (2016). "Duterte's Resurgent Nationalism in the Philippines: A Discursive Institutionalist Analysis." Retrieved from https://journals.sagepub.com/doi/10.1177/18681034160350030 4

Fatih Ozturk, Serdar Malcoc, Arife Figen Ersoy. (2016). "Patriotism as Perceived by Social Studies Teachers: An Outlook on the Individual, Society and Education." Retrieved from https://www.researchgate.net/publication/312525254_Patriotis m_as_Perceived_by_Social_Studies_Teachers_An_Outlook_o n_the_Individual_Society_and_Education

Johanna Marie Castillo, Conrad Gian Fario, Jean Andre Trinidad, Racidon Bernarte. (2016). "National Pride of the Filipino Youth." Polytechnic University of the Philippines. Asia Pacific Journal of Multidisciplinary Research. 4(3).

Wai-Chung Ho. (2016). "A Comparative Review of Music Education in Mainland China and the United States: From Nationalism to Multiculturalism." Retrieved from https://files.eric.ed.gov/fulltext/EJ1106482.pdf

Michael Their. (2016). "Maturing Measurement: Valdity and Reliability – Trials of a Measure of Global Citizenship for High School Students." University of Oregon.

Jingxiang Wang and Shaoying Jia. (2015). "The Contemporary Value of Patriotism." Beijing Union University, Beijing, China.

CHAPTER III

RESEARCH METHODOLOGY

This chapter presents the research techniques employed including research designs, methods, and procedures, research setting, population, data analysis, and technique used to interpret the data.

RESEARCH DESIGN

This study used the qualitative design to determine the students' level of performance in the manner of writing, singing, and understanding of the Philippine National Anthem. Observation, writing, singing, and focused group discussions and verifications of concerned students, teachers were done. Therefore, a narrative inquiry and phenomenological analysis were chosen to present the subject of inquiry.

METHODS AND PROCEDURES

As soon as the proposed title was accepted by the panel members of the School of Graduate Studies, the researcher prepared a request letter to conduct the study from the Schools Division Superintendent Dr. Mariano B. De Guzman of Naga City Division and Schools Division Superintendent Dr. Loida N. Nidea of Camarines Sur Division.

Upon the approval of the request letter, the researcher made the schedule to visit the respondents' schools.

The researcher conducted an observation of the Flag Ceremony with every Monday schedule in every school. Observation instruments were also prepared; selected teachers and students who were present during the Flag Ceremony were requested to answer the form. After which, with the approval of the school head, the researcher requested selected students to write the lyrics of the Philippine national anthem with a given time frame of five (5) to seven (7) minutes. In addition, two to three students were also requested to sing the Lupang Hinirang in a capella. With the approval also of the school head, the researcher invited two teachers from the school who will attend the Focused Group Discussion in one venue only. Students from Sipocot National High School were personally invited by the researcher with the consent of their parents. All the respondents from five schools attended the Focused Group Discussion in the same schedule and venue. The venue was personally requested by the researcher with the approval of the school head and guidance counselor of the school. The researcher invited an expert to serve as the facilitator to conduct the Focused Group Discussion. A scheduled Focused Group Discussion was prepared and served as an actual analysis of the study. During the FGD, Narrative Inquiry and Phenomenological Analysis used as a method when students and teachers narrated their personal experiences and their analysis on the writing, singing, and understanding of the Philippine National Anthem.

RESEARCH SETTING

The observation, writing, and singing were conducted in the four (4) selected schools of Division of Camarines Sur: Sipocot National High School, Sta. Lutgarda National High School, Milaor National High School, and Calabanga National High School, and one (1) school from Schools Division of Naga City, the Camarines Sur National High School. These schools were selected due to their conduct of the Philippine National Anthem since most of the schools were not already conducting the Flag Ceremonies. It is because the Department of Education issued the DepEd Memorandum # 10, s. 2015 postponing all off-campus activities and other school activities that require mass gathering due to the novel coronavirus (2019-nCoV). The researcher was able to select four (4) big schools in the Division of Camarines Sur and the biggest school in the Naga City Division. However, the Focused Group Discussion was only conducted in Camarines Sur National High School with an allotted time of one and half hours. Every school was represented by two teachers. In addition, nine (9) students also attended from the two schools only. The whole duration of the data gathering started from January to March 2020.

POPULATION

The respondents of the study during the conduct of observation of the flag ceremony were twenty-four (24) teachers and students coming from the five selected schools. Seventy-five (75) students wrote the lyrics of the Philippine national anthem with fifteen (15) representative students in each school. Thirteen (13) students were also requested to sing individually. During the Focused Group Discussion, ten (10) teachers attended represented by five (5) schools; and nine (9) students were also present.

Participants were students and teachers from the selected secondary school from Division City School of Naga, Camarines Sur National High School, and selected schools from the Division of Camarines Sur: Sipocot National High School, Sta. Lutgarda National High School, Milaor National High School, and Calabanga National High School.

DATA ANALYSIS AND TECHNIQUE

To organize the data, narrative inquiry and phenomenological analysis were used as a method. Themes identification is one of the most fundamental tasks in qualitative research. Developing common themes or patterns that intersect the data was the primary method of data analysis. In making themes for the data, responses were utilized.

The identified themes of the data were aligned and answered the research questions. The thematic presentation was used in this study through presentation, analysis, interpretation, and linkages per theme.

The thematic presentation was used as a way to gain understanding from data gathered on writing, singing, and understanding of Bicolano learners in the Philippine national anthem.

Descriptive statistics such as percentage and ranking were used to determine the indicators in the manner of writing, singing, and knowledge of the Philippine National Anthem.

NOTES

George Ferguson and Yoshio Takane. (1989). Statistical Analysis in Psychology and Education., 6th ed. Singapore: McGraw Hill Company.

Jerilyn P. Magdaong. (2014). "Teachers' Multiple Intelligence and Students' Performance in Music, Arts, Physical Education and Health." Unpublished Master's Thesis. University of Nueva Caceres, Naga City.

CHAPTER IV

ANALYSIS AND INTERPRETATION

This chapter contains the presentation, analysis, and interpretation of the data gathered in this study. A narrative inquiry and phenomenological analysis were chosen to present the subject of inquiry. It used the qualitative design to determine the students' level of performance in the manner of writing, singing, and understanding of the Philippine National Anthem. Observation, writing, singing, and focused group discussions and verifications of concerned students and teachers were done.

PERSONAL EXPERIENCES OF BICOLANO LEARNERS AND TEACHERS IN PHILIPPINE NATIONAL ANTHEM

With the conduct of the Focused Group Discussion, Observation on Flag Ceremonies, Individual Singing and Writing of the National Anthem in the Division of Camarines Sur and Division of Naga City, the researcher was able to collect responses which were converted into indicators and helped to identify the personal experiences of Bicolano learners and teachers in writing, singing, and understanding of the Philippine National Anthem.

A. Writing. Table 1A presents the concise summary of the indicators generated from the responses of the personal

experiences of Bicolano learners and teachers in writing the Philippine National Anthem. Indicators generated were spelling, phrasing, and alignment of writing the Lupang Hinirang. Among the three indicators, writing in terms of phrasing had the most number of correct responses with 13.33%, followed by alignment with 5.33%. Least among the indicators is writing along with spelling with no students who got a perfect score (0.00%). Some of the misspelled terms were the following:

(1) Silanganan was written as silangan, sinilang, sinilangan, simong alab, silang alang, sinangalan, lasinglangalan, sinag ng araw, sinagalan, selangan, sinalagan, and sinang alan; (2) Dibdib – digadib, didi, digdib, diddid, dipdip; (3) Mo'y – mong, mo; (4) Buhay – bughaw, bunghaw, boghaw, bughay, hilaw; (5) Magiting – magising, magiliw, awitin, magitin; (6) Manlulupig – mang lolope, man lulupid, mang lulupid, mang lulupin, mang lolopit; (7) Pasisiil – masisiil, masisiit, madidiig, pasisiit; (8) Dagat – daga't, dilakad; (9) Bundok – mundo, mudo;(10) Simoy – simo'y, simuy, sinag; (11) Mong – moy, mo, mo'y (12) Dilag – dalag, dalaga, dilagang, dalagang; (13) Paglayang minamahal – baying minamahal, may minamahal, mayang minamahal, aming minamahal, paglayang di matataw, taglayang minamahal, batlayang minaminal; (14) Nagniningning – nagsisiil, magniningning; (15) Niya – na, nang, ng; (16) Luwalhati't – luwalhatit, luhalti't, walhati't, huwal'hatit.

In terms of phrasing, "Bayang magiliw" ranked as the easiest phrase while "Aming ligaya na pag may mang-aapi"

Table 1A

THEMES ON PERSONAL EXPERIENCES OF BICOLANO LEARNERS AND TEACHERS IN WRITING THE PHILIPPINE NATIONAL ANTHEM

Aspect	Indicators	Responses
Writing	Spelling	16 out of 84 terms in Lupang Hinirang were identified as difficult for the students to spell
	Phrasing	"Bayang magiliw" ranked as easiest phrase; "Aming ligaya na pag may mang-aapi" ranked as the most difficult phrase
	Alignment	50.67% write the first stanza of the song
		32.00% write the second stanza of the song
		13.33% write the third stanza of the song
		6.67% write the fourth stanza of the song
		Nobody completely write the song

ranked as lowest. With the alignment of the song, the first stanza was the highest while nobody completed the lyrics of the national anthem.

Based on the gathered data, results showed that students do not know the proper spelling of some of the lyrics of Lupang Hinirang. There was no student who writes the lyrics perfectly. A response from a student has a significant answer why there is a failure in the writing manner of the Pambasang Awit, she claimed,

> *"Nagpasurat pong lyrics samuya yung teacher, tapos pigrecord na po…… Si teacher*

mi po garo mayo sya pakiaram po, and kan pinacheck mi po ang notebook namin dun sa tigsurat mi po, binilugan nya lang po yung maling lyrics po, and 'di nya naman po pigsabi na dapat ito, dapat ito, silanganan bakong sinilangan."

(Our teachers requested us to write the lyrics, then it was recorded... Our teacher, as if, he doesn't mind, and the time that he checked our notebook, he just encircle the incorrect lyrics, but he did not explain anything, that this should be the right term, silanganan, not sinilangan)

There was no follow-up given to the students on their errors and until such time they went home, nobody corrected their spelling and terms. On the other hand, phrases also of Lupang Hinirang were not properly written. Based on the results, it showed that students have a minimal idea of how to write the phrasing of the national anthem. They write the song in a paragraph manner which must be in poetic form since it is originally written as a poem. A response from a student revealed why there is a failure in writing the phrasing. It was pointed out that teachers did not explain the meaning of each line and stanza and meanings were based on their own understanding. Data also showed that the majority of the students commit mistakes in the alignment of the song. Their songs were written not in a style of poem writing but in paragraph style which does not have meter, rhyme, and stanza. Students were given a time frame of five minutes to completely write the song, however, it was clearly observed that they find this as difficult activity because there were no subjects in their school focusing on the proper writing and alignment of the lyrics. While writing, some of the students are looking above or merely close their eyes while murmuring and softly singing the lyrics of the Lupang Hinirang. The researcher also witnessed how the students had difficulties in writing even the spelling of the song. Some of them asked their classmates about the proper spelling of the term. It was also specified that even teachers have problems in terms of writing the song through a response:

> *"I agree. I cannot write it alone".*
> *"Kinakanta ta pa sa isip." "Di mo sya masusurat*
> *na without singing."*
>
> *(You cannot write it without singing)*

Spelling, as the lowest among the three indicators, attributed to the reason that no subject in schools focuses on the proper writing and discussion of terms in the national anthem. Teachers at the elementary level, let the pupils copy the lyrics on the board and there was no follow-up given to them afterward. However, deeper issues on teaching the National Anthem were discovered when teachers expressed their disappointment on the new curriculum that there were no competencies related to teaching how to write properly the "Lupang Hinirang". According to them, it was just their initiative to request each student to write the lyrics of the National Anthem. Issues were thoroughly answered why there is a failure in writing the spelling of the terms. It was recommended that teachers should check the spelling of the Lupang Hinirang every time they require their students to write

the national anthem. Each term should be explained to the student so that students will understand even the deep Filipino terms. The curriculum along the Philippine culture and the arts must also review, for the students to develop their love for the country. Topics on the modules and books in any subjects especially in MAPEH and AP must restore the value of love for the country especially the topic on the Philippine National Anthem as one of our national pride. Another recommendation disclosed that lyrics and importance of the National Anthem and other national symbols should be taught in the MAPEH subjects since the teaching of the Philippine National Anthem in MAPEH was already removed in the curriculum and topics focused more on Asian and Western music and arts, and therefore, following the competencies given, there were no outputs and activities related to the Philippine National Anthem. It was also recommended that the Department of Education must also restore the signing of the clearance before the school year ends to enable teachers to have a hold on the students to require them to perfectly write the spelling of the lyrics of the Philippine National Anthem.

Reyes (2019) agreed with the findings on the difficulty of the students in writing the lyrics of Lupang Hinirang. He pointed out that when teachers ask the students to write the lyrics down, one would always hear students humming the tune. Students do not memorize the lyrics by reciting them like prose or poem. Teachers always say that a Filipino should know the lyrics by heart, soul, and mind without having to hum the tune during writing. In another recent article (Tan, 2018), it was discussed that the most difficult term revealed "luwalhati" does not appear in the early versions of the Lupang Hinirang. Luwalhati is a joy made ebullient by the love put in serving other people. It then refers to emotions that go outward or, more specifically, a joy that moves outward. It is the opposite of dalamhati. Our national anthem is not just joyful, but romantic. The replacement of the word "niya" with either "nang" or "niya't" is another common error written by the students. Students replace some words with similar-sounding ones (Wikipedia, 2020).

B. Singing. Table 1B presents the summary of responses of Bicolano learners and teachers in singing the Philippine National Anthem. Thirteen (13) students from five different schools were requested to sing the Philippine National Anthem and among these students, no one pronounced perfectly the terms of the Lupang Hinirang. There were five indicators generated namely: Pronunciation, Mastery, Sincerity, Rhythm and Tempo, and Pitch and Melody. Among all the responses, students who sing National Anthem with few mistakes have the highest criterion with 30.76%, followed by students not placing their hands on their chest properly, 23.07%. Least among the criteria during singing is the Filipino pronounced well the terms when singing with 0.00% and students in proper pitch and tune with a percentage of 7.69. Data revealed that some students pronounced the lyrics of the "Lupang Hinirang" depending on how they know and memorize the terms. Teachers noticed that students only murmur during the singing of the Philippine National Anthem and words were not properly and clearly pronounced. These are indicators that students do not pronounce the lyrics properly.

Table 1B

THEMES ON PERSONAL EXPERIENCES OF BICOLANO LEARNERS AND TEACHERS IN SINGING THE PHILIPPINE NATIONAL ANTHEM

Aspect	Indicators	Responses
Singing	Pronunciation	Filipino words was pronounced well while singing
	Mastery	Students sings national anthem with few mistakes
		Students and teachers memorized the national anthem
	Sincerity	Students not paying attention while singing
		Students not placing their hands in their chest
		Not looking at the Philippine flag
	Rhythm and Tempo	Time signature and wrong conducting
		Teachers and students changed the tempo of the Lupang Hinirang
	Pitch and Melody	Students in proper tune while singing

During the conduct of individual singing, terms like "pasisiil" was pronounced "masisiil", "dilag ang tula" pronounced as "dalagat tula", "silanganan" pronounced as "silangalang", "manlulupig" was "manglulupig", "buhay became buhaw", "l'walhati't" pronounced as "luhalhati't", "dilag" pronounced as "dila".

Students relied on what they heard in the music, not knowing the words that they are singing were not correct. Yet, practice makes perfect. Daily singing makes you more familiar with the song. However, this saying does not apply in the singing of the Lupang Hinirang. Philippine National Anthem is taught as early as the child goes to school. Teachers let the pupils read the lyrics and hear the music inside the classroom. It is done in community singing and not by one on one instruction. During high school level, it is implied that students mastered the Lupang Hinirang since it is part of their everyday lives as a student. However, teachers observed that their students do not know the National Anthem. The researcher also personally observed that singing the National Anthem during flag ceremonies was done for compliance only. During the conduct of the observation, it was stated by the observers that students are not singing during flag ceremonies. Without the accompaniment of the DXC or recorded music, students' voice during singing is very soft. There are also students who continuously sing even though they do not totally memorize the lyrics.

> *Majority of the observers identified that students has problems in terms of mastery of the song. It was also noted that students sing the National Anthem without showing their love and pride for the country. They do not focus on the singing; rather, they are chatting and whispering with each other. It was observed that students lack discipline and do not care in the ceremony. They don't look at the flag anymore while singing.*

These are some of the indicators that students nowadays only sing the Philippine National Anthem because it is part of the schools' routine. It was also confirmed by the students that not focusing during flag ceremonies showed disrespect to the National Anthem. Another indicator is being familiar with the rhythm and tempo of the "Lupang Hinirang". It is very important to facilitate not only the singing but also in leading the class or students. The teacher who is conducting has a very important role during the Flag Ceremonies. One of the factors associated is the conductor leading the National Anthem. It was brought out that teachers nowadays do not want to lead in front because of the bullying and criticisms in terms of how the teacher conducts the beat of the national anthem. It was observed that most of the teachers conducting the Lupang Hinirang don't know how to conduct properly the song. They claimed that some of the teachers were quite dancing while conducting and do not really know the proper way of conducting the beat. Students confirmed these statements that teachers have a very big impact on their attitude and behaviour during flag ceremonies. They admitted that their focus was transferred to the manner of conducting and sometimes on the negative matter of the conductor. It was also cleared out that the Pambansang Awit ng Pilipinas is originally in march tempo, and must be performed and sung in march tempo. It was discussed during the Focused Group Discussion that the original time signature is 2-4 according to the musical composition of Julian Felipe. However; if it is sung in *a capella*, it can be conducted in a 2-4 time signature. Manner of a proper way of conducting was also explained and demonstrated by one of the music teachers. He explained that in conducting lessons, conducting must be beyond the horizon of the conductor's eye, conducting in choir, band, and community singing are different.

> *It was also observed by music specialist that*
> *on the last part of the song, singers slowly sings the*
> *part "Lupa ng araw ng l'walhati't pagsinta, buhay*

ay langit sa piling mo; Aming ligaya na 'pag may mang-aapi, ang mamatay ng dahil sa'yo". He pointed out that no ritardando (gradually slowing) on the last part and singing must be in the original tempo until on the last note.

When the time signature and tempo change, the conducting of such a song will also change. It is the responsibility of the teacher-conductor who leads during the Flag Ceremony on how the students will sing and react to the elements of the music. Based on the responses of the teachers and students, there is a problem in terms of the conducting and it was also confirmed by the students. Another important element in music is the melody of the Lupang Hinirang.

During the Flag Ceremony, the teacher-conductor will give the pitch when she sings "Bayang magiliw". But students will sing the Lupang Hinirang using different pitches.

It is very important that the pitch given by the teacher must be followed since it is a community singing. Some students sang the "Lupang Hinirang" and it is obvious that they sang the "Lupang Hinirang" not in correct pitch and melody. There are students who sing the Lupang Hinirang in a high pitch, some are in a low pitch, making different pitches when singing. Students were also requested to sing the Lupang Hinirang and one of the participants was asked about his observation on the singing of the students if it is correct or not. Based on the technicalities of the music, there are students who

sing the national anthem as if they were just only reading a sentence. Based on the observation conducted by the researcher, it was found out that most of the students do not sing the proper rendition of the song. There were students who only mumble the lyrics, just like they were just reading a story, and some sang the national anthem out of tune. In community singing like the conduct of flag ceremonies, Filipinos as a whole are singing in unison depending on the tune provided by the conductor and song leader. However, most of the students are not singing properly the national anthem and not taking it seriously, that is why most of the students and Filipinos do not master the melody of the song.

Teaching the right pronunciation of the lyrics of the Lupang Hinirang was not given priority by the teachers because they also follow a set of competencies in their subjects. Students failed in pronunciation during the singing of the National Anthem. Teachers are aware of this situation, but because there are a lot of lessons that need to be finished and it is not in the curriculum per se, most of the teachers neglect to teach the proper pronunciation and lyrics of the song. It was not also checked by the teachers how the students pronounced the terminologies as long as the students join in the singing of the Lupang Hinirang. No follow-up was given to the students in the right pronunciation. Based on the solo singing performed by selected students, it was clearly revealed that pronunciation of the students is failing. It was also found out that most of the students do not know how to properly sing the national anthem. Some of them do not master the lyrics, some are singing out of tune, and some have problems with both the music and lyrics.

In addition to this, Flag Ceremony was also conducted once a week since it was indicated in the Section 17 of RA 8491. With this, students only sing the Philippine national anthem every Monday sometimes with the accompaniment of music or a band. It was opposite with the Flag Ceremonies five years ago that Lupang Hinirang is sung every day since flag ritual is conducted in schools every day. Mastery means the rendition of the national anthem aligned with the Republic Act 8491 known as the Flag and Heraldic Code of the Philippines. Based on the gathered data, it can be concluded that students nowadays lack discipline and attitude towards their attendance during Flag ceremonies. It is considered by many as just a routine activity in schools and students attended "just for compliance only". It should not be viewed this way; since this activity trains the child to learn discipline and this provides motivation and direction to Filipinos' character development and love for our flag, national anthem, and other national symbols. They symbolize our national ideals and aspirations, without which we cannot control. To summarize the declaration of principles in Republic Act No. 8491, our flag, national anthem, and national symbols manifest our virtues as a people and inculcate the minds and hearts of our native land. As Filipino citizens, let the song stir your heart and mind what we can do to our country; don't just mouth the lyrics by rote. The observations also revealed that teachers were being bullied and subjected to criticism when they lead the Lupang Hinirang because all eyes were focused on them. The manner of conducting, the physical appearance, and the issues in his life were brought out when he is seen in front. Such bullied

statements and manner were sometimes posted on Facebook and other social media accounts. It was added that even students do not want to go in front because they feel the same impression with the teachers. Students feel that they are bullied when they are in front of their schoolmates that is why they also do not want to lead the Panatang Makabayan and Panunumpa. Teachers admitted that personally, they do not want to lead in conducting especially if they are not Music or MAPEH teachers. It is the task of the teachers to ensure that the students are singing the song in a right pitch with pride and dignity as a Filipino. However, it was found out that teachers do not mind if the students are singing out of melody. In this situation, it was recommended that teachers must dissect the lyrics of the national anthem for the students to understand all the terms present in the song since there are many unfamiliar terminologies in the Lupang Hinirang. Let also the students repeat all the terms that were not familiar to them so that they will pronounce it properly when they sing the song. Before the end of the school year, teachers should require the students to sing the song to check if they really memorize the Philippine national anthem. Daily singing of the national anthem will also increase the mastery of the song. Revisit the curriculum and increase the topics focusing on the country as a whole and there should be an integration of music, culture, and arts along all learning areas. Schools must advocate cultural education since the problem lies not only in the national anthem but also in the promotion of Filipino tradition, culture and arts. Teachers must intensify the integration of DepEd core values in teaching their lessons as part of the evaluation proper. It was also recommended that corporal punishments must be restored but in moderation so that students will behave properly and well-disciplined. Teachers should also collaborate and teach those who do not know how to conduct so that they will not be bullied or criticized. Teachers should also require their students to sing in a correct pitch after they memorize and master the national anthem. It is also a task of every teacher to correct the mistakes of their students since evaluation, assessment, and remediation is part of the lesson plan and therefore teachers must prepare a rubric with regards to the performance of the students in singing the Lupang Hinirang.

Tan (2013) also pointed out that Filipinos especially children sung the national anthem "Sa dagat at bundok, sa simoy at sa langit mo'y bughaw, May dilag ang tula, at awit sa paglayang minamahal; Ang kislap ng watawat mo'y tagumpay na nagniningning, Ang bituin at araw na, kalian pa ma'y di magdidilim". She even reiterated that after years of assembling at the school's grounds, after hundreds of Lupang Hinirangs sang during flag ceremonies and injecting patriotism into children's hearts, brains and veins, lyrics are still distortedly sung by Filipinos. The House Bill 5224 is about the correct rendition of the national anthem "Lupang Hinirang" and requiring everyone to sing along when it is played in public. All students at public and private schools would also be required to memorize the anthem. The bill also cleared out that during the conduct of flag raising and lowering, all persons must stand at attention facing the Philippine flag, if displayed, or the band or conductor; civilians salute the flag with their right palm over the left chest as a sign of respect. Filipinos

would be required to sing the national anthem and to do with enthusiasm. This bill is flexible to all religious beliefs. However, they must show full respect, by standing at attention. Failure to sing the national anthem with insufficient energy would be punishable by up to year in prison and a fine of P50,000 to P100,000 pesos. A second offense would include both a fine and a prison time, and violators would be penalized by "public censure" in a newspaper. "The singing shall be mandatory and must be done with fervor", the bill states. In addition to this, the bill specifies the proper rendition of "Lupang Hinirang" in accordance with the musical arrangement and composition of Julian Felipe: 2-4 beats when played, within the range of 100 to 120 metronome, in 4-4 beats when sang. Schools would be required to ensure to follow this tempo. National Historical Institute filed a complaint to the Filipinos for changing the tone and tempo of the Philippine National Anthem. Arnel Pineda, a renowned singer who sang the Philippine National Anthem during the boxing competition of Manny Pacquiao, started well in the song but faltered when he tried to raise the pitch of the final part of the anthem. He was called by the National Historical Commission either. It was also pointed out by Campillan (2017) that Filipinos must be proud of our heritage and culture. Teachers should inculcate into the minds of the students not just the lyrics but also the whole point why the need to give respect to the flag and the national anthem. She even compared Filipinos to foreigners whose pride is evident each time their national anthem is played in public.

C. Understanding. Table 1C presents the data along understanding aspect. Among the eleven generated responses, love for the country is integrated among subjects in schools is the highest with 83.33%, followed by Makabayan as one of the core values of the Department of Education, 77.77%. Least among the parameters is not standing straight and having unnecessary movements during flag ceremonies, 16.67%.

Table 1C

THEMES ON PERSONAL EXPERIENCES OF BICOLANO LEARNERS AND TEACHERS IN UNDERSTANDING THE PHILIPPINE NATIONAL ANTHEM

Aspect	Indicators	Responses
Understanding	Patriotism	Love for the country is integrated among subjects in schools
		Makabayan as one of the core values of the Department of Education
	History of the national anthem	No subjects focusing on teaching the history of the Philippine national anthem
		Teaching the history of the anthem is not present in the competencies and curriculum
	Respect in Philippine flag and anthem	Not standing straight and having unnecessary movements
		Continuously walking or doing what they are doing though national anthem is played
		Students wearing their caps
		Students are using their gadgets and having their headphones on
		Teachers communicating with each other
		Laughing and bullying the national anthem
	Filipino culture and values	Parents teaching their children about love for the country
		Home correction on singing the Philippine national anthem

Based on gathered responses, teaching patriotism and love for the country is quite diminishing. The removal of the Philippine history subject in secondary schools since the school year 2014-2015, when it introduced the K-12 curriculum also weakened the patriotism and nationalism of the learners. There is also an absence with the integration of teaching patriotism, loyalty to the nation, and promotion of indigenous materials in schools so it is very hard for the students to appreciate the Filipino culture, arts, and history. The Makabayan as one of the core values of the Department of Education remains unexplained to the students during discussions. It was just recited during the conduct of flag ceremonies but it was not expounded and integrated into subjects in schools. Memorizing the national anthem is very hard for the students though they sing it every day in schools during flag ceremonies wherein students sang and stood at attention because teachers let the students copy the lyrics and memorize the song; however, there is no time for discussion of it. They let the students sing with the recorded music but proper singing was not really taught inside the classroom. These are some of the indicators that there is a failure in teaching the Philippine National Anthem. However, teachers claimed that they are not teaching the national anthem because it was not in the curriculum per se, and supposedly it was taught during the primary years of the students in school. Some of the teachers gave little time for teaching national anthem because they observed that their students do not know the Lupang Hinirang, but limited time only was given to this topic since it is not part of the curriculum and competencies in their subject should be finished within the quarter. It was also found out that only Grade 7 has Philippine music lessons. However, Philippine National Anthem is just a part of the topics of the First Grading and just a sort of review to the students. It is because students were expected to master Lupang Hinirang during the primary level. They explained that in Music subjects, Music 7 focuses on the Cordillera, Visayas, and Mindanao Music. As the students moved on to the next grade level, the emphasis of the topics are Asia, American, Europe, and World art, culture, literature, and history. The history of the Philippines is taught as a unique narrative of colonialism, reaction, and revolution. History allows the Filipinos to see beyond textbooks and see the past through new lenses. Studying history allows people to gain valuable perspectives on the problems of modern society. Music and lyrics of the Philippine national anthem are taught in schools, but little about its history. Late novelist Crichton stated in his famous saying "If you don't know your history, you don't know anything".

> *Students stated that although it was not part of their lessons, some of their teachers briefly discuss the history of the Lupang Hinirang, although it is a very critical lesson that students must understand. It was also pointed out that even private schools weakened the teaching of the Philippine national anthem.*

National Anthem is a symbol of what our heroes did to fight for Philippine independence and a symbol of being a Filipino. Based on the responses above, there is a little

observation on teaching the history of the song. It was not explained well to the students the importance of each stanza, and how it is related to the history of the Philippines during the time of the Philippine revolution. Little did that teachers focus on how the Lupang Hinirang became the national anthem of the Philippines. Respecting the national anthem and other national symbols were part of the lessons taught during elementary days. Pupils were taught by their teachers the importance of giving respect, honor, and reverence to these national pride to instill in the minds and hearts of every Filipinos the people who have fought to achieve the freedom of our country. But for some reason now, this national pride has been taken for granted by some Filipinos of no particular ages.

In an observation conducted by students and teachers to different schools, it was found out that most of the students and even teachers do not respect the Philippine National Anthem and Philippine flag. Students continuously walking and doing something in their respective buildings even if they heard the Lupang Hinirang, some passed by and they don't stop to partake in the activity. Some boys are wearing their caps during the flag-raising/lowering, some are using their gadgets secretly with the headphones on, listening to music on their cellphones, talking to each other and then they laugh at some students who are out of tune. It was also observed that on the last part of the song, students sung the last line "Ang mamatay ng dahil sa'yo" in a very loud voice then they laugh as if they are making fun of the song. In addition to this, even teachers do not behave properly during the conduct of flag ceremonies. There are those who are chatting with each other and not partaking in the activity.

These observations were also complemented by the teachers during the Focused Group Discussion. Majority of the observations during the flag ceremony were chatting with each other during the singing of the Philippine National Anthem. During the flag-raising and lowering, everyone must stop doing anything and pay attention to the singing of Lupang Hinirang. However, these responses do not conform with what the Filipinos should do. However, discipline, fulfilling duty towards nation, decent manners and behaviour should not only be taught in schools, but it should also start at home. The first school of a child is his home where he first learnt things that help him to lead a good life later on. Toddlers and pre-schoolers were taught nursery songs and the Philippine National Anthem sometimes taught by mothers at home. One of the students claimed that her mother was the one who taught her the national anthem. In an early stage, Lupang Hinirang was first learnt at home. It was also identified that behaviour and discipline were first experienced at home,

"Siguro ang una dapat i-mould sa bata ay behaviour." "Nagsisimula yan sa bahay. Kung ano ugali ng bata pagpasok nya, nagrerepresent kung anong discipline ang binigay sa loob ng bahay. Home discipline. Home factor." (Maybe the first

thing that should be mould to every child is his behaviour. It begins at home. What behaviour the child has in school, it is the representation of the discipline that he has in his home. Home discipline. Home factor).

Moreover, teachers are one of the most important factors contributing to student learning and achievement. They play also an important role in moulding the behaviour and respect of the students.

Respect in the national anthem, flag, and other national symbols is quite diminishing. Filipinos have been taught to be respectful the day they learned to speak their first words. It is one of the most unique characteristics of a Filipino, and even foreigners can commend the respectfulness of Filipinos. However, it was noticed that being respectful of Filipinos weakened as time goes by. As Filipinos, it is our responsibility to respect our national anthem, flag, and other national symbols. But, actions like wearing caps/hats, laughing while singing, not putting their hands on their chest, and not looking at the Philippine flag are some of the indicators that Filipinos are taking for granted their attendance during the flag ceremonies. Students nowadays are attending the flag ritual ceremonies but they were not seriously taking part in the activity. Based on the responses above, students and teachers do not behave properly during the conduct of the Philippine national anthem. For them, this is their time to chat with each other and talk about their lives. It serves as their meeting place. During the singing of Lupang Hinirang, the focus of the students and teachers are not on singing but on their conversations. Using of gadgets and earphones was obvious that they tend to listen to other music on their cellphones. It was a disrespectful act on the Philippine National Anthem. Students who are taking part in flag ceremonies merely stand silently, often not even at attention instead of singing loud and proud as Filipinos. There is also a relation between the attention that Filipinos are giving to the anthem and who is the conductor and how he is conducted in front. Programs and activities were begun with the national anthem sometimes with the choir, rondalla, band, audio-visual activities, and other manner which catches the attention of the audience. Because of the presence of the accompaniment of the DXC, some students don't sing the anthem. It implies that Filipinos are mesmerized by the videos and performers that sometimes accompany the playing of the national anthem, filled with images of actors, actresses, heroes, and sceneries. These performers catch the attention of the Filipino people and don't focus on the singing of the anthem, therefore, the spirit of patriotism has gone. Majority of the Filipinos, even at small private gatherings, are loath to singing the Pambansang Awit. They are taking for granted their attendance during the singing of the Philippine National Anthem and there is a minimal amount of respect to the national pride and symbols. There are still students who continue walking and doing what they are doing even the national anthem was heard. Moreover, not only students are doing it, even bystanders and professionals. The love for the country is best manifested in how Filipinos respect the flag and anthem. In international events like the Boxing Competition of

Manny Pacquaio, most of the singers and performers sung the Philippine national anthem, not in its proper rendition and some of the singers changed the lyrics of the Lupang Hinirang. If Filipinos cannot respect their own flag and anthem, and cannot behave properly during the conduct of flag ceremonies, perhaps, foreigners globally will also not respect what's ours. Global citizenship begins with self-awareness. Self-awareness also enables individuals to identify the national identity and the responsibility towards the country. The little respect that Filipinos have for these national symbols shows how little respect they have for anything. Based on the responses given, students do not have the interest in the national anthem. It is concluded that based on the combined findings during individual writing, individual singing of the students, and responses during the FGD, minimal students only memorize the correct lyrics and rendition of the song. According to the students, it is because they are more focused on social media like Facebook, Messenger, Instagram, and others. However, it was suggested that these sites can help young individuals to learn about Philippine national pride through creating blogs, posts, and videos about the national anthem, flag, and other national symbols. During the first meetings of the school year, teachers must spend ample time teaching Lupang Hinirang through writing, singing, and listening to it. In addition to this, parents can also help teachers teach their kids since cultural beliefs, values, norms, knowledge practices, experiences, and cultural expressions were first developed at home and children's learning is grounded in the unique perspective and principle of culture. Proper rendition of the song, behavior, and discipline while singing the song can be taught first at home, and must be experienced at home. Parents must be hands-on on their child's learning. It is not only the work of the teachers to teach children. The saying "It takes an entire village to educate a child" means it must be a partnership effort of the home, school, and community to teach a child discipline, behaviour, and patriotism. It will be continuously taught at schools where culture-based education develops the students to instill a sense of national pride. It was also recommended that students must be obliged to understand the Philippine national anthem by stressing out the correct title and rendition of the song. Teachers can also integrate the history of the national anthem and how the Katipuneros fought for Philippine Independence in teaching their lessons in Filipino, Araling Panlipunan, Music, and Arts. Demonstrate the pride in being a Filipino by being in the proper disposition during the flag ceremony as one of the manifestations in the Makabayan core value of the Department of Education. In this manner, students will develop a healthy personal and national self-identity that has been the aim of Philippine education and global citizenship. Social media like Facebook, Twitter, and Instagram can also be a strategy to help young individuals to learn about national pride by creating blogs, posts, and videos about the national anthem, flag, and other national symbols.

Campillan (2017) stated her disappointment when the essence of paying respect, patriotism, and pride to the Philippine National Anthem had long gone. She even compares her experiences during an early age that are still vivid in her mind that even vehicles show reverence by stopping. Passersby also halt and look at the flag with the highest esteem possible. In the same manner, Araneta (2018) said that one historian expressed his dismay when he went to an SM mall to watch a particular movie. When the recorded voice announced that Pambansang Awit is about to be played, nobody stood up except his family. Everyone was seated as if they had not heard the announcement and were patiently waiting for the movie to start. He could not help but feel irritated by the cavalier disregard of the national anthem, so he exclaimed to the audience in an authoritarian voice. It was invoked through a relatively obscure law in a 2018 incident in San Fernando, Cebu, where two bus drivers sped off while the town's local officials were holding a flag ceremony (Bunya, 2019). The drivers were apprehended and required to make a public apology and were also suspended by their respective employers. Also in 2018, police in Lemery, Batangas, arrested 34 moviegoers who refused to stand up during the singing of the national anthem. Another alarming issue was the video uploaded on a social media platform showing a man dancing while the national anthem was being played. The National Historical Institute called the attention and issued a notice to Fil-am Youtuber Bretman Rock, who is based in Hawaii, and reminded the public that dancing to the national anthem is a violation of the flag and heraldic code. Former President Fidel Ramos signed into law the Republic Act 8491 on February 12, 1998, the Flag and Heraldic Code of the Philippines, which states the guidelines and proper way of displaying and hoisting the Philippine flag. In this act, it must be noted that when the national anthem is played, men should remove their hats or headdresses with the right hand and hold them at the left chest. Women should salute by placing the right hand over the left chest. Section 21 of the Republic Act 8491 clearly stated that during the flag-raising ceremony, the assembly shall stand in formation facing the flag. At the moment the first note of the anthem is heard, everyone in the premises shall come to attention; moving vehicles to stop. Flag raising ceremonies are sometimes taken for granted. It was pointed out at Balugto news that the spearheading brass band or chorale or rondalla takes away the accountability of the attendees to sing the Lupang Hinirang. The would-be singers become the audience to the 'performers'. This scenario also happens during the program when multi-media take the course of singing the Lupang Hinirang and the majority of the audience simply wait until the last note is played. Buan (2013) suggests that schools should properly educate their students whenever and wherever the national anthem is played. The parents should also remind their children to stand at attention. Paras (2016) cleared out that teachers shall inculcate patriotism and nationalism and appreciate the role of national heroes in the historical development of the country as part of the Article XIV Section 3 of the 1987 Philippine Constitution. According to her, there are numerous activities in schools that can develop and instill the patriotism of the learners. She also added that singing of the national anthems should be taught regularly and explain patriotic words and terms to further develop their patriotic sentiments. K-12 without a strong cultural base will never become meaningful and relevant. Without cultural roots, without cultural memory, without cultural soul, our educational

system will fail, for in these cultural essentials, we find meaning in being a human member of human and humane society. (Lopez, 2018). It was stated by Isip (2015) that one of the reasons why most Filipino citizens do not memorize the lyrics of the Lupang Hinirang because they were not passionately taught and supervised during their formative years of schooling. As a preventive measure and remedy of producing an ignorant Filipino, teachers, as well as parents, should go hand and hand in patiently teaching the correct lyrics and rendition of the song. It was cleared out that teachers should also oblige every pupil to memorize the lyrics of the Lupang Hinirang by stressing out the correct title and rendition of the song during their MAPEH, or music subjects. Filipinos tend to sing it from memory and know so little about its history (Tan, 2018). There are many who still refer to the anthem as "Bayang Magiliw" which are indeed the first two words of the song but not the title. National anthems are important, something taught to us early in life. It is a symbol of who we are, of what happened in the past, and what it represents for us. Bedruz (cited by Gozo, 2018) emphasized the importance of revisiting the history of the flag and be reminded of how our heroes fought for our independence. The flag reminds us that we must uphold their values and continue their legacy. Jarabelo also stressed out that national pride should be given importance for it reflects the love for country, and it is one of the ways to value the sacrifices of the people who died protecting our motherland.

HEIGHTS OF HONOR: STRENGTHENING OUR NATIONAL SYMBOL

Patriotism is a love for one's country for no other reason than being a citizen of that country. It is a common virtue that pertains to the love for a nation, with more emphasis on values and beliefs.

Knowing the national anthem and showing how it is properly sung is one way of displaying respect and love for the country. However, in research conducted, it was found out that students' patriotism is diminishing while assessing their writing, singing, and understanding of the Philippine national anthem.

As a preventive measure and remedy of producing ignorant Filipino citizens in the future, teachers, as well as the parents, should go hand in hand in patiently teaching the love for the country to their kids. In addition to this, teachers from pre-elementary to high school or even colleges and universities should spend ample time not only in teaching the Lupang Hinirang but oblige every student to memorize the lyrics of the song by stressing out the correct title and rendition of the national anthem during their Araling Panlipunan, MAPEH, or Music subjects. Thus, making every Filipino citizen realize that memorizing the National Anthem is a duty and responsibility to our country.

In order to bridge the gap between the findings and recommendations of the study entitled Narratives of Bicolano Learners on Patriotism: Basis for the Development of Instructional Material Promoting National Pride, a module was developed which aims to cultivate and develop patriotism and love for the country. The module was personally designed with discussions, lectures, and activities that will engage teachers and learners in proper dissemination of information about the Philippine National Anthem. The researcher thought of activities that would fit into the level of primary and secondary students who have difficulties in writing, singing, and understanding of the Philippine National Anthem. After finishing the module, it will be brought to the MAPEH Supervisors of the Division of Naga City, Dr. Joseph N. Condeno, and Division of Camarines Sur, Mrs. Imelda A. Nardo for validation and evaluation of the material. With their approval, the material can be used by the teachers and learners within the Division of Naga City and Division of Camarines Sur as a reference in teaching the Philippine National anthem. Eventually, learners will be able to have insights about the proper writing, singing, and understanding of our national pride, Lupang Hinirang.

NOTES

Gillian Reyes. (2019). "Appreciating the Filipino Identity Through our Literature and Culture." Retrieved from https://www.rappler.com/voices/ispeak/appreciating-filipino-identity- through-literature-culture

https://en.wikipedia.org/wiki/Lupang_Hinirang

Sheenah Tan. (2013). "With Fervor: Lupang Hinirang like how it should be at present." Retrieved from https://www.newsgra.ph/1838/risktalkers-fervor-lupang-hinirang/

Leila Cruel. (2018). "Perpetuate and honor the Philippine national anthem." Retrieved from
https://www.change.org/p/to-the-people-of-the-republic-of-the-philippines-perpetuate-and-honor-the-philippine-national-anthem

Llanesca Panti. (2018). "Historian says changing last lines of Lupang Hinirang." Retrieved from https://www.google.com/amp/s/www.gmanetwork.com/news

"The Filipino Spirit." (n.d.). Retrieved from http://msc.edu.ph/centennial/anthem.html

Jose Abeto Zaide. "The Evolution of Lupang Hinirang."(2017). Retrieved from

https://news.mb.com.ph/2017/06/29/the-evolution-of-lupang-hinirang/

Ambeth R. Ocampo. (2014). "Lupang Hinirang or Bayang Magiliw." Philippine Daily Inquirer. Retrieved from https://opinion.inquirer.net/72558/lupang-hinirang-or-bayang-magiliw

Matthew Zapruder. (n.d.). "Poetry on the Brink." Retrieved from
http://bostonreview.net/forum/poetry-brink/difference-between-poetry-and-song-lyrics

Jan Arcilla. (2020). "Teachers urge DepEd to Teach Philippine History in Basic Education." Retrieved from https://www.manilatimes.net/2020/03/05/campus-press/teachers-urge-deped-to-teach-philippine-history-in-basic-education/700210/

Rhoda G. Campillan. "Respect for the Philippine National Anthem." Borderless. Retrieved from https://www.panaynews.net/borderless-respect-for-the-philippine-national-anthem/

"Students' Opinions about the Daily Flag Ceremony." Retrieved from
https://spgsped.wordpress.com/2014/07/29/students-opinions-about-the-daily-flag-ceremony/

Froilan G. Isip. (2015). "Philippine National Anthem: Bayang Magiliw?." Sun Star Pampanga.Retrieved from https://www.pressreader.com/philippines/sunstar-pampanga/20150325/281625303796790

Michael Tan. (2018). "Revolution, love, joy." Retrieved from
https://opinion.inquirer.net/113227/revolution-love-joy

Jonnel Gozo. (2018). "Why should we respect the Ph flag?." Retrieved from
https://www.rappler.com/move-ph/171219-respect-philippine-flag-aguinaldo-shrine

Niña Jean Jarabelo.(n.d.). Retrieved from https://www.academia.edu/36247925/CHAPTER_1-INTRODUCTION

Patricia A. Bunya. (2019). "With Fervor." Philippine Daily Inquirer. Retrieved from https://opinion.inquirer.net/120591/with-fervor

Gemma Cruz Araneta. (2018). "Embarassed to be Filipinos."Retrieved from https://news.mb.com.ph/2018/05/08/embarrassed-to-be-filipinos/

The Singing of the Philippine National Anthem. (2018). Retrieved from Balugto.

http://balugto.blogspot.com/2018/01/the-singing-of-philippine-national.html

Cesar Apolinario. (2015). "Of courage and fervor: Honoring our   nation, respecting its symbols." GMA News Online. Retrieved from
https://www.gmanetwork.com/news/lifestyle/content/500 014/of-courage-and-fervor-honoring-our-nation-respecting-its-symbols/story/

Ferdinand M Lopez. (2018). "Philippine Culture-Based Education: Responding to the Challenges of a Nationalist Education."Retrieved   from http://web.nlp.gov.ph/plcon2018/sites/default/files/philippine_c ulture-based_education.pdf

Arthur Buan. (2013). "Stop the disrespect for Lupang Hinirang."   Retrieved   from https://opinion.inquirer.net/47679/stop-the-disrespect-for-lupang-hinirang

"Flag   Ceremony   in   Schools."   Retrieved   from https://steemit.com/steemiteducation/@muhammadan/flag-ceremony-in-schools-832f077baf972

Daniel Victor. (2017). "Philippines May Get New Law: Sing National Anthem with Spirit or Face Prison Time." The New   York   Times.   Retrieved   from https://www.nytimes.com/2017/06/27/world/asia/philippines-may-get-new-law-sing-national-anthem-with-spirit-or-face-prison-time.html

"The Philippine flag: why and how we should respect it." (2013). Sun Star. Retrieved from https://www.sunstar.com.ph/article/289005

"How Well Do you Know the Philippine National Anthem."(n.d.). Retrieved from http://driftwoodjourneys.com/how-well-do-you-know-the-philippine-national-anthem/

https://www.youtube.com/watch?v=VPvuFmfN0AI
https://www.youtube.com/watch?v=UE8XL4_XLJ0
https://www.youtube.com/watch?v=uOgXBBigds0
https://www.youtube.com/watch?v=uOgXBBigds0

CHAPTER V

SUMMARY, CONCLUSIONS, AND RECOMMENDATIONS

This chapter presents the summary of findings, conclusions, and recommendations of this study on the national pride of Bicolano learners. It answered the following:

OBJECTIVE 1:

To narrate the personal experiences of the Bicolano learners and teachers in writing, singing, and understanding the Philippine National Anthem using the Narrative Inquiry and Phenomenological Analysis.

FINDINGS

1. Along writing aspects, writing in terms of phrasing had the most number of correct responses with 13.33%, followed by alignment with 5.33%. Least among the indicators is the writing along spelling with no students who got a perfect score (0.00%).

2. Along singing, thirteen (13) students from five different schools were requested to sing the Philippine National Anthem and there were five indicators generated namely: Pronunciation, Mastery, Sincerity, Rhythm and Tempo, and Pitch and Melody. Among all the responses, students who sing

the national anthem with few mistakes have the highest criterion with 30.76%, followed by attitude and discipline while singing with 23.07%. Least among the criteria during singing is the Filipino pronounced well the terms when singing with 0.00% and students in proper pitch and tune with a percentage of 7.69.

3. Among the eleven generated responses in understanding aspect, love for the country is integrated among subjects in schools is the highest with 83.33%, followed by Makabayan as one of the core values of the Department of Education, 77.77%. Least among the parameters are students' behaviour during flag ceremonies, 16.67%.

CONCLUSIONS

1. Students were better at writing the phrasing of the song Lupang Hinirang since they are familiar with writing poems and songs. However, they are weak in spelling because teachers let the pupils copy the lyrics, there was no follow-up given to them after requiring them to write the song, and no subjects in schools focusing on teaching the proper writing of the national anthem.

2. Students can sing the Lupang Hinirang from start-up to the end since it is sung almost every day even during their primary years of schooling. On the other hand, the right pronunciation of the lyrics of the Lupang Hinirang is failing and most of the students do not know the proper pronunciation of the terms in the song because it was not given priority by the teachers in

schools with the reason that they also follow a set of competencies in their subjects.

3. Students are aware of the national pride and symbols of the Philippines because it is taught in schools. Teachers taught the relevance of the Filipino culture, tradition, and the arts to the present times. However, many youths today have unnecessary behaviour while singing during flag ceremonies. Students are attending the flag ritual ceremonies but they were not seriously taking part in the activity, they merely stand silently, often not even at attention instead of singing loud and proud as Filipinos. They are taking for granted their attendance during the singing of the Philippine National Anthem and there is a minimal amount of respect to the national pride and symbols. There are still students who continue walking and doing what they are doing even the national anthem was heard. Moreover, not only students are doing it, even bystanders and professionals.

RECOMMENDATIONS

1. Teachers should check the spelling of the Lupang Hinirang every time they require their students to write the national anthem and each term must be explained to the student so that students will understand even the deep Filipino terms. National anthem should be taught to MAPEH subjects to restore the value of love for the country and signing of monitoring slips or clearance before the school year ends, should also restore to check if the student can write properly the Lupang Hinirang.

2. Teachers should check the lyrics of the national anthem for the students to understand all the terms present in the song. Let also the students repeat all the terms that were not familiar to them so that they will pronounce it properly when they sing the song. Before the end of the school year, teachers should require the students to sing the song to check if they really memorize the Philippine national anthem. Daily singing of the national anthem will also increase the mastery of the students singing the song. It was recommended to revisit the curriculum and increase the topics focusing on the country as a whole and there should be an integration of music, culture, and arts along all learning areas. Schools must advocate cultural education since the problem lies not only in the national anthem but also in the promotion of Filipino tradition, culture and arts. Teachers must intensify the integration of DepEd core values in teaching their lessons as part of the evaluation proper. It was also recommended that corporal punishments must be restored but in moderation so that students will behave properly and well-disciplined. Teachers should also collaborate and teach those who do not know how to conduct so that they will not be bullied or criticized. Teachers should also require their students to sing in a correct pitch after they memorize and master the national anthem. Teachers must prepare a rubric with regards to the performance of the students in singing the Lupang Hinirang.

3. Filipinos must display their respect for the national anthem and encourage others to stop and partake in the flag ceremonies. Teachers must spend ample time teaching Lupang Hinirang through writing, singing, and listening during the first

meeting of the school year. Proper rendition of the song, behaviour, and discipline while singing the song can be taught first at home, and must be experienced at home. It will be continuously taught at schools where culture-based education and the significance of Makabayan core values develop the students to instill a sense of national pride. It must be a partnership effort of the home, school, and community to teach children discipline, behaviour, and patriotism. Students must be obliged to understand the Philippine national anthem by stressing out the correct title and rendition of the song. Teachers can also integrate the history of the national anthem and how the Katipuneros fought for Philippine Independence in teaching their lessons in Filipino, Araling Panlipunan, Music, and Arts. Social media like Facebook, Twitter, and Instagram can also be a strategy to help young individuals to learn about national pride by creating blogs, posts, and videos about the national anthem, flag, and other national symbols.

OBJECTIVE 2.

To develop a module promoting national pride.

The module was developed which aims to cultivate and develop patriotism and love for the country. It was designed with discussions, lectures, and activities that will engage teachers and learners in proper dissemination of information about the Philippine National Anthem. It can be used by primary and secondary teachers in teaching the Philippine National Anthem. Eventually, learners will be able to have insights about the proper writing, singing, and understanding of our national pride, "Lupang Hinirang".

BIBLIOGRAPHY

A. BOOKS

Ferguson, George, and Takane, Yoshio. (1989). Statistical Analysis in Psychology and Education. 6th ed. Singapore: McGraw Hill Company.

Winold, Allen. (1966). Elements of Musical Understanding. New Jersey: Prentice Hall, Inc.

B. JOURNALS/PERIODICALS

Castillo, Johanna Marie., et.al. (2016). "National Pride of the Filipino Youth." Polytechnic University of the Philippines. Asia Pacific Journal of Multidisciplinary Research. 4 (3).
Nair, Subadrah Madhawa and Rajeswary P. Sinasamy. (2017). "Patriotism among Secondary School Students and Its Relationship with their Interests towards Learning History." Asian Journal of Education and Training. 3 (2); 110-117.

Pineda, Haidee C. "The Arts and Philippine Studies." UPDate Magazine. 4(1);18.

C. UNPUBLISHED MATERIALS

Magdaong, Jerilyn P. (2014). "Teachers' Multiple Intelligence and Students' Performance in Music, Arts, Physical Education

and Health." Unpublished Master's Thesis. University of Nueva Caceres, Naga City.

Their, Michael. (2016). "Maturing Measurement: Validity and Reliability – Trials of a Measure of Global Citizenship for High School Students." University of Oregon.

D.   ELECTRONIC SOURCES

Apolinario, Cesar. (2015). "Of courage and fervor: Honoring our nation, respecting its symbols". GMA News Online. Retrieved June 8, 2015, from https://www.gmanetwork.com/news/lifestyle/content/500014/of-courage-and-fervor-honoring-our-nation-respecting-its-symbols/story/

Araneta, Gemma Cruz. (2018). "Embarassed to be Filipinos." Retrieved May 11, 2018, from https://news.mb.com.ph/2018/05/08/embarrassed-to-be-filipinos/

Arcilla, Jan. (2020). "Teachers urge DepEd to Teach Philippine History in Basic Education." Retrieved March 5, 2020 from https://www.manilatimes.net/2020/03/05/campus-press/teachers-urge-DepEd-to-teach-philippine-history-in-basic-education/700210/

Bernardo, Allan B.I. (2017). "Exploring Political Values of Filipinos Using an Etic Approach." University of Macau. Retrieved from https://www.pap.org.ph/sites/default/files/upload/pjp2017-50-

2-pp7-38-bernardo-exploring_politicalvalues _of_ filipinos_using_an_etic_approach.pdf

Buan, Arthur. (2013). "Stop the disrespect for Lupang Hinirang. " Retrieved from https://opinion.inquirer.net/47679/stop-the-disrespect-for-lupang-hinirang

Bunya, Patricia. (2019). "With Fervor." Philippine Daily Inquirer. Retrieved April 6, 2019, from https://opinion.inquirer.net/120591/with-fervor

Campillan, Rhoda G. "Respect for the Philippine National Anthem". Borderless. https://www.panaynews.net/borderless-respect-for-the-philippine-national-anthem/

Cepeda, Mara. (2017). "How to sing PH National Anthem, and Display Symbols in Proposed Flag Code." Retrieved June 30, 2017, from https://www.rappler.com/nation/house-bill-penalties-wrong-use-lupang-hinirang-flag-symbols
Costelo, Margaret Louise. (2009). "The Filipino Ringside Community: National Identity and the Heroic Myth of Manny Pacquiao." Retrieved from https://repository.library.georgetown.edu/bitstream/handle/108 22/552909/costelloMargaret.pdf?seq

Cruel, Leila. (2018). "Perpetuate and honor the Philippine national anthem." Retrieved from https://www.change.org/p/to-the-people-of-the-republic-of-the-philippines-perpetuate-and-honor-the-philippine-national-anthem

De Leon, Janice Ponce. (2018). "Filipinos Parade their Patriotism, Positive Spirit." Retrieved from https://gulfnews.com/going-out/society/filipinos-para de-their-patriotism-positive-spirit-1.2237250

DepEd. (2018). "Briones: Strengthening Global Citizenship Key to Achieving Education Goals 2030." Retrieved from https://pia.gov.ph/news/articles/1012912

"DO 50, s. 2015 – Observance/Conduct of Flag Raising and Lowering Ceremonies and Proper Sequence in Official DepEd Programs Involving Singing of the Philippine National Anthem."(n.d.).   Retrieved   from. https://www.deped.gov.ph/2015/10/29/do-50-s-2015-observance-conduct-of-flag-raising-and-lowering-ceremonies-and-proper-sequence-in-official-deped-programs-involving-the-singing-of-the-philippine-national-anthem/

Druckman, Daniel. (2010). "Nationalism, Patriotism, and Group Loyalty: A Psychological Perspective." Retrieved from http://bev.berkeley.edu/Ethnic%20Religious%20Conflict/Ethnic%20and%20Religious%20Conflict/2%20National%20Identity/Druckman%20nationalism.pdf

"Filipino National Anthem – Chosen Land (Commonwealth Era)." Retrieved from https://lyricstranslate.com/en/national-anthems-filipino-national-anthem-chosen-land-commonwealth-era-lyrics.html

"The Filipino Spirit." (n.d.) Retrieved from http://msc.edu.ph/centennial/anthem.html

"Five Characteristics of Poetry."(n.d.). Retrieved from https://quizlet.com/22300934/five-characteristics-of-poetry-flash-cards/

"Flag Ceremony in Schools."(n.d.). Retrieved from https://steemit.com/steemiteducation/@muhammadan/flag-ceremony-in-schools-832f077baf972

Gozo, Jonnel. (2018). "Why should we respect the Ph flag?." Retrieved from https://www.rappler.com/move-ph/171219-respect-philip pine-flag-aguinaldo-shrine

"HB 5224." (January 31, 2017). Retrieved from http://www.congress.gov.ph/legisdocs/first_17/CR00163.pdf

Hernandez, Butch. (2016). "A Better, Safer and Kinder Nation." Philippine Daily Inquirer. Retrieved from https://opinion.inquirer.net/95678/a-better-safer-and-kinder-nation

https://en.wikipedia.org/wiki/Lupang_Hinirang

https://www.pinterest.ca/pin/359162139016177981/
https://en.wikipedia.org/wiki/Lupang_Hinirang#/media/File:Sheet_Lupang_hinirang.jpg
https://languages.oup.com/google-dictionary-en/
https://www.youtube.com/watch?v=41guxaNk9FY
https://www.youtube.com/watch?v=ufmqINWdGg4

https://edicio.wordpress.com/2013/07/13/dekada-70-and-imagined-communities/

https://www.slideshare.net/AchesJolieto/core-values-70992478

https://1.bp.blogspot.com/-0KhZTPWDglk/XaNTvpElB9I/AAAAAAAC7RM/2YR8Xkr HdQYgcfVJU4Jk9CM46xwSs9mDgCLcBGAsYHQ/s1600/20191013_211652.jpg

https://www.youtube.com/watch?v=VPvuFmfN0AI

https://www.youtube.com/watch?v=UE8XL4_XLJ0

https://www.youtube.com/watch?v=uOgXBBigds0

https://www.youtube.com/watch?v=uOgXBBigds0

Ho, Wai-Chung. (2016). "A Comparative Review of Music Education in Mainland China and the United States: From Nationalism to Multiculturalism." Retrieved from https://files.eric.ed.gov/fulltext/EJ1106482.pdf

"How Well Do you Know the Philippine National Anthem."(n.d.). Retrieved from http://driftwoodjourneys.com/how-well-do-you-know-the-philippine-national-anthem/

Isip, Froilan G. (2015). "Philippine National Anthem: Bayang Magiliw?." Sun Star Pampanga. Retrieved from https://www.pressreader.com/philippines/sunstar-pampanga/20150325/281625303796790

Jarabelo, Niña Jean.(n.d.). Retrieved from https://www.academia.edu/36247925/

"Legarda Encourages Filipino Youth to Emulate Rizal's Patriotism, Love for Culture and Environment."(June 19, 2018.)Retrieved from http://www.senate.gov.ph/press_release/2018/0619_legarda1.asp

Llego, Mark Anthony. "DepEd Core Values Indicators: Concrete Manifestation." Retrieved from https://www.teacherph.com/deped-core-values-indicators-concrete-manifestation/

Lopez, Ferdinand M. (2018). "Philippine Culture-Based Education: Responding to the Challenges of a Nationalist Education." Retrieved from http://web.nlp.gov.ph/plcon2018/sites/default/files/philippine_culture-based_education.pdf

"Lupang Hinirang." (n.d.). Retrieved from https://en.wikipedia.org/wiki/Lupang_Hinirang

Mathene, Neal D. (2014). "Naming the Artist, Composing the Philippines: Listening for the Nation in the National Artist Award." Retrieved from https://escholarship.org/content/qt5bc31081/qt5bc31081.pdf

"National Anthem."(n.d.). Retrieved from https://nhcp.gov.ph/resource/national-anthem/

Nepomuceno, Priam. (2019). "Mandatory ROTC Necessary to Instill Patriotism Among Youth." Philippine News Agency. Retrieved from https://www.pna.gov.ph/articles/1061627.

Ocampo, Ambeth R. (2014). "Lupang Hinirang or Bayang Magiliw." Philippine Daily Inquirer. Retrieved from https://opinion.inquirer.net/72558/lupang-hinirang-or-bayang-magiliw

Ozturk, Fatih, et. al. "Patriotism as Perceived by Social Studies Teachers: An Outlook on the Individual, Society and Education." Retrieved from https://www.researchgate.net/publication/312525254_Patriotism_as_Perceived_by_Social_Studies_Teachers_An_Outlook_on_the_Individual_Society_and_Education

Pangilinan, Ching. (2018). "Cultivating Patriotism." Sun Star Pampanga.Retrieved from https://www.sunstar.com.ph/article/1747239

Panti, Llanesca. (2018). "Historian says changing last lines of Lupang Hinirang." Retrieved from https://www.google.com/amp/s/www.gmanetwork.com/news

Paras, Maria Jonelle T. (2016). "Inculcating Patriotism among Learners." Sun Star Pampanga. Retrieved from https://www.pressreader.com/

Patajo-Katipunan, Lorna. "Criminalizing 'not singing with fervor'!." Retrieved from https://businessmirror.com.ph/criminalizing-not-sing ing-with-fervor/

"The Philippine flag: why and how we should respect i.t"(June 12, 2013). Sun Star.Retrievded from https://www.sunstar.com.ph/article/289005

"Proclamation No. 1239." (n.d.). Retrieved from https://www.lawphil.net/executive/proc/proc2016/proc_1239_2016.html

Reyes, Gillian. (2019). "Appreciating the Filipino Identity Through our Literature and Culture."Retrieved from https://www.rappler.com/voices/ispeak/appreciating-filipino-identity-through-literature-culture

"Republic Act 8491."(n.d.). Retrieved from https://www.officialgazette.gov.ph/1998/02/12/republic-act-no-8491/

Rocamora, Joyce Ann L. (2018). "OFWs: Modern-day Heroes Still." Philippine News Agency. Retrieved from https://www.pna.gov.ph/articles/1046084

Sardoc, Mitja. (2017). "The Anatomy of Patriotism." Retrieved from https://www.researchgate.net/publication/317688502_The_anatomy_of_patriotism

"The Singing of the Philippine National Anthem." (January 13, 2018). Balugto. Retrieved from http://balugto.blogspot.com/2018/01/the-singing-of-philippine-national.html

"Students' Opinions about the Daily Flag Ceremony."(2014). Retrieved from https://spgsped.wordpress.com/2014/07/29/students-opi nions-about-the-daily-flag-ceremony/

Tan, Michael. (2018). "Revolution, love, joy." Retrieved from https://opinion.inquirer.net/113227/revolution-love-joy

Tan, Sheenah. (2013). "With Fervor: Lupang Hinirang like how it should be at present." Retrieved from https://www.newsgra.ph/1838/risktalkers-fervor-lupang-hinirang/

Teehanke, Julio C. (2016). "Duterte's Resurgent Nationalism in the Philippines: A Discursive Institutionalist Analysis." Retrieved from https://journals.sagepub.com/doi/10.1177/18681034160350030 4

Victor, Daniel. (2017). "Philippines May Get New Law: Sing National Anthem with Spirit or Face Prison Time." The New York Times. Retrieved from https://www.nytimes.com/2017/06/27/world/asia/philippines-may-get-new-law-sing-national-anthem-with-spirit-or-face-prison-time.html

Wai-Chung Ho. (2016). "A Comparative Review of Music Education in Mainland China and the United States: From Nationalism to Multiculturalism."Retrieved from https://files.eric.ed.gov/fulltext/EJ1106482.pdf

Wang & Jia. (2015). "The Contemporary Value of Patriotism." Retrieved from https://file.scirp.org/pdf/AASoci_2015051414401558.pdf

Zaide, Jose Abeto. (2017). "The Evolution of Lupang Hinirang." Retrieved from https://news.mb.com.ph/2017/06/29/the-evolution-of-lupang-hinirang/

Zapruder, Matthew. "Poetry on the Brink." Retrieved from http://bostonreview.net/forum/poetry-brink/difference-between-poetry-and-song-lyrics

ABOUT THE AUTHOR

JERILYN M. TORIO, Ed. D

The youngest among the three children of Mr. & Mrs. Edgar L. Magdaong, she spent her childhood days at Lupi, Camarines Sur. In her young mind, she knows exactly the importance of education instilled by her parents which were both teachers in public schools.

She graduated her baccalaureate course at Philippine Normal University with the degree of Bachelor of Secondary Education Major in Music Education in 2007 as Cum Laude. She

obtained her post-graduate studies at the University of Nueva Caceres where she graduated her Master of Arts in Education Major in Educational Management in 2014 and Doctor of Education Major in Educational Management in 2021.

She taught music subjects in the regular and business high school department of the University of Perpetual Help System DALTA from 2007-2011 and was the pianist and trainer of rondalla and anklung ensemble. Currently, she is a Master Teacher I at Sipocot National High School; the proponent of the schools' Special Program in the Arts Curriculum and designated as the Cultural Coordinator.

Being part of the Camarines Sur Teachers' Choir, she managed to sing with the group in different events and competitions. The group was awarded with Gold and Silver Medal at the 4th International Choral Competition held at Lake Toba, Indonesia. She is one of the Division resource speakers in Music and is also a writer and quality assurer of the modules in Music subjects used in the junior high school of the Division of Camarines Sur. She is also an editor of some of the Music modules in Grade 4 which can be downloaded from DepEd LRMDS.